CONTENTS

INTRODUCTION

There is so much in adult life that you can only know if someone has explained it to you, and it can be scary and confusing when you are expected to just understand things. When I first started posting videos on TikTok, I was initially answering questions about cleaning, but very quickly I started being asked about so many things that were completely unconnected to cleaning, from break-ups to politics, and so I thought I would write this book to try to give you all some answers.

When you are a child, the world just happens around you – the lights stay on (or not, as not all parents can always manage that), people tell you where to go and what to do, and food either happens or it doesn't. Some of you will have grown up in a world that ran seamlessly in the background: you probably went shopping with your parents, and heard them talk about bills, but you didn't pay much attention. Some of you will have experienced an absence of that, however, such as parents who didn't pay bills, who didn't buy food very often, whom you never watched clean and tidy, and who never explained anything much at all. You will all have learned some things – children always do – but once we grow up and leave home, whatever our childhood experience, we all find we have massive gaps in our knowledge.

Not everyone has parents to ask, and not all parents can give answers to questions – and, yes, the internet is a marvellous place, but we all know that there is downright dangerous information out there, and if your starting point is that you know nothing about something, it's often impossible to work out if you've been given good, safe information or are being fed a pile of dangerous nonsense.

We all have massive holes in our knowledge – how would you know about sweeping chimneys, for example, if you've never lived somewhere with a fireplace? Maybe you've never needed to know the current laws relating to rental properties. And who do you ring when your neighbour starts shouting at his hedge? We aren't born just knowing these things, and when you first leave home, you've not had a chance to learn – the old saying 'you don't know what you don't know' holds absolutely true.

In this book, I've tried to cover all the main things I think you might need to know. I've also explained where to look and how to find reliable information about all the many things I cannot cover in this one slim volume!

I've gone through all my content to get an idea of the most-often-asked questions, and I've also asked my TikTok followers what people want to know. I hope we can all agree that there are no stupid questions. Some subjects are covered in more than one chapter, because if you need to use this book as a quick reference as and when you need it, I suspect it will be handy to be able to dip in and out rather than having to read the whole thing!

I would also like to point out that I'm giving you the advice I have given my own children. I've tried to ensure it is accurate, but obviously I'm not a qualified psychologist, say, or a trained plumber, and I cannot stress enough that sometimes the adult thing to do is to ask a proper expert – I might be able to tell you how to wire a British standard plug, but for the love of heaven, PLEASE ask a certified electrician to rewire your house. Knowing when to seek help is important!!!

Throughout this book you'll often find me urging you to look online – firstly, because sometimes a video demonstration is clearer than I can be in writing, and also because you can often get a more in-depth view of what you are looking for. Be careful about the source, though. As I've mentioned, there is a lot of misleading and often flat-out wrong information to be found online.

For health-related matters, the NHS website gives good up-to-date information; likewise, www.gov.uk is an accurate and up-to-date source of information on many other subjects. Laws change, and medical advice gets updated regularly, so learning to find the most reliable sources is a valuable lesson.

If you are unsure who to contact about a problem, it's worth ringing your local council and asking. They can point you in the right direction for all sorts of things, from housing issues and pests to noise problems. But I will also put a list at the end of the book of links and resources that you might find useful (see p. 295).

Look for people with proper knowledge in their field – not just influencers, but verified tradespeople, proven cooks, etc. I see so many people giving advice that is quite frankly dangerous, all while claiming to be an expert, so do check that any qualification they claim to have comes from an accredited body.

After all, we've all seen the raw milk, anti-vax influencers and the like, and while it's easy to laugh at them, these ideas are gaining traction – and they have the potential to be lethal. Learn to check information like this with trusted sources, and be very wary indeed about those who tell you NOT to trust doctors or scientists. There is a pernicious strain of anti-intellectualism spreading worldwide and it is extremely dangerous. The people who remember what life was like before vaccines and antibiotics are getting old and dying, so there is now a gap where unscrupulous people can squeeze in to make a quick buck. Life was NOT some wonderful utopia in the past – do not let yourself get sucked in.

I've interspersed all my advice throughout with examples of how I myself have coped with different issues – good, bad and amusing – to try to stop things becoming dry and boring. Also, I wanted to let you know you are not alone if you are overwhelmed by all the stuff you don't know. My first flat had a very expensive water heater, for example, so I avoided using it – and then couldn't work out why my plates and glasses wouldn't come clean. I honestly didn't understand that I needed properly hot water – so I simply threw all the plates and glasses away. My neighbour, meanwhile, couldn't ever get the washbasin in her room clean; she tried washing-up liquid and a cloth, and yet it remained disturbingly grubby. So she painted it with a tin of white gloss paint! To be fair, when the paint started to peel off (about three days later), it did indeed take the dirt with it, but I'm afraid the basin remained awful for months afterwards.

The world has changed a lot since I left school, and you might find it interesting to understand how things used to be done. I find that sometimes this knowledge can help make sense of how things are done now. This is another trap for the unwary – the often-pushed idea that things were better in the past, that people back then had some ancient wisdom that we should return to. There is some truth in that – learning to darn a sock and sew on a button is going to save you money – but pasteurisation, for example, saved hundreds of thousands of lives.

As you get older, your experience grows, and we learn from our mistakes – or we hope to. But no one can know everything. We all need advice and guidance as we go through life. I certainly do.

I had no idea when I first went out into the world, and, as I had no one to ask, I made some epic mistakes. I still do, for that matter. You too will make mistakes, as did your parents or caregivers, but I'd like to think having a book like this might help make this whole adulting thing a little less terrifying. Obviously, you will read some things in the chapters that follow and feel I am stating the obvious, but quite often things are only obvious if you know them, so, if that's the case, just move swiftly on to the next bit while muttering under your breath.

Perhaps that will be the very first thing for us to take on board – no one is always right. Every single human who ever lived is fallible. We all make mistakes: it's normal and it's okay. Admit you were wrong, do your best to sort out the error, and move on. Getting it wrong only becomes a problem if you either cannot or will not learn, and therefore continue to make the same mistake again and again.

1

PACKING UP AND MOVING OUT

So you're moving out to set up on your own – either permanently, or just to university for term time, and it's daunting. The first thing to do, of course, is find some-where to live.

Types of accommodation

University halls vs private rentals

Universities have halls of residence, but many students live in house shares, and, sadly, many unsavoury landlords try to take advantage of students and put them in unsafe and poorly maintained places. The university and your parents or guardians may be able to help by directing you to the right people and making sure you're safely and legally housed. Not everyone will have that option, though – many parents are so out of touch they struggle with the basics, and plenty more aren't bothered about being involved.

Types of house shares

Flats and houses are extortionate to rent solo, so it's unlikely you'll be able to afford to live on your own. It's more likely you'll rent a room in a house share. There are mostly two sorts of house shares. The first one is where a bunch of friends club together and rent a house. They are all named on the tenancy document and are all liable – if one moves out, you need to get the document amended. If not, and you just drift off, you may find in a year's time you are being chased for back rent or the electricity bill if the others don't pay. I live like this, but the two other named tenants are two of my adult children.

The other is an HMO (house in multiple occupation), where each of you has a room you rent from the land-lord, and each of you has a separate contract with him or her. These MUST be registered as HMOs, and the law around them is slightly different. You should have a key for your bedroom door, but facilities such as the kitchen and bathroom will often be shared. If you want to move out, you must tell your landlord, giving the required notice, and then he or she is responsible for renting out your old room – in other words, it has no effect on the other tenants.

The logistics: deposits, credit checks and guarantors

If you are renting, you will need to put down a deposit against damages, and your landlord will run a credit check and often ask for references and a guarantor. A guarantor is someone who agrees to cover any financial liability if you are unable to pay. If you wreck the house, run up huge bills or vanish into the night, your landlord can (and – I cannot stress this enough – WILL) chase your guarantor for the money. It makes for an extremely tense Christmas dinner if your grandparents have just had a bill for six thousand pounds on account of a party that got out of hand.

Your deposit must, by law, be put into a deposit scheme, and you must be given details of which one your landlord has used (see p. 13 for more information about this).

Remember your rights (and your responsibilities) as a tenant

You have rights as a tenant, and those rights will depend on what kind of tenancy you have. As I write this, there is a possibility of a renter's reform bill that will update the current laws on renting, and which will hopefully give more protection to renters. Please look up those rights, as they will change over time, and make sure the information is reputable – a .gov.uk suffix means you're getting the latest information from the government. There are some important things to be aware of from the beginning, though.

According to the housing justice charity Shelter, to comply with the law, your house or flat should meet the following criteria:

— It should be free from damp.

— It should not have an unsafe layout – for example, you should not have a door opening to a drop, or a stair you have to go on hands and knees to ascend (both of which I have seen).

— It should have natural light – if not, then enough lighting should be available.

— It should be well ventilated.

— It should have both hot and cold water.

— It should have drainage, and a loo and basin accessible.

— It should have facilities for the preparation of food, and somewhere to dispose of waste.

Basically, the house must be fit for human habitation. You might have to share a loo and a bathroom, but they must be easily accessible.

You cannot just be locked out of your home – either with your belongings dumped on the doorstep or still inside. If this happens, GO TO THE POLICE. Quite often, the police will try to avoid helping by saying it is a 'civil matter', but it absolutely is their job to get you safely back into your home (see also p. 251). Once you're back inside your room, it's up to you and your landlord to sort things out, but it's pretty obvious that at this point you need legal advice, ideally from a solicitor. Please bear in mind that solicitors do charge money, but if you have an obviously winnable case, they may agree to represent you on a 'no win, no fee' basis. This term comes from the fact that, in civil cases, the loser is usually ordered to pay the legal costs incurred by the winner meaning your landlord would have to pay their fees, but if your solicitor loses the case, you would not be charged. If a solicitor thinks they have a good chance of winning, they are often prepared to take the gamble.

If your room or flat is unsafe, does not have a smoke alarm or a carbon monoxide alarm, or is damp, mouldy or otherwise unfit for human habitation then Shelter, Citizens Advice and very often your local council are the places to go for help or advice (see list on p. 295).

Like your landlord, you too have legal responsibilities in your new home. You must keep it in good condition, for example. You're allowed to be untidy, but you must not allow your lifestyle to damage the landlord's property. So keep it clean, keep your landlord informed of repairs that need doing. My landlord is my neighbour and is stellar, but it's just easier for all concerned if I handle the small stuff. I do not ever do any job involving the electricity or the water, though, because if I make a mistake I risk severe damage to the property.

You have to let your landlord, or their agent, or those they have asked to do repairs, into the property – IF they give you at least twenty-four hours' notice. You can ask them to reschedule if it's inconvenient, but you cannot just flatly deny access. However, if they start looking through your possessions or making unreasonable demands (asking you not to cook certain foods, for example, or to stop doing anything that does not put their property at risk), then perhaps seek help. If you have a letting agent, it's worth starting with them – complain that your landlord keeps harassing you. If that's no good, speak to Citizens Advice or perhaps Shelter. Your landlord cannot just let themselves in without notice at any time, but, if they notify you on Monday that they are arriving on Friday to inspect the house and you don't reply, the chances are they will just let themselves in if you don't answer the doorbell. There is a thing known as 'quiet enjoyment' when renting. This is the idea that you should be able to live somewhere without your landlord harassing you. This is enshrined in law (Jenkins vs Jackson, 1888, in case you want to know) and it states that a tenant must be able to live in peace without unnecessary disturbance from the landlord or their agents.

Avoiding scams and bad rentals

Do not pay a fee just to view a property, as it may well be a scam. It's surprising how many times a flat that has had its details posted somewhere, such as Rightmove.co.uk, will then be offered on Facebook by scammers. Another trick used by scammers is to demand rent upfront – for the first six months or year, only for their victims to discover that the flat was never theirs to rent, and they've scarpered with a small fortune. Using a reputable agent with premises you can visit, and one with online reviews, will help avoid this. And make sure you look at the property in person if possible (of course, if you live in London and are moving to Edinburgh, that's obviously not as feasible). Look in cupboards, and peer closely at new paintwork to see if they've just painted over damp.

A cautionary tale: a friend recently rented a freshly painted room. In hindsight, we should have realised something was wrong, as the shower room was neither clean nor freshly painted. After a week, the paint smell faded, the smell of damp crept in, and two months later the room was black with mould. I think my friend first realised he'd made a mistake when he went to get a fob for the door and was handed a cockroach trap, and asked if he'd seen any rats in the kitchen.

Look for the fuse box to see if it looks in reasonable repair and that it's a modern one compliant with regulations. Is there a smoke alarm and a carbon monoxide alarm installed? Is the place reasonably clean. Use your nose and have a good sniff – can you smell anything unpleasant? If you get a chance, speak to other tenants or neighbours to see if they know anything about the place.

There are Facebook groups for people seeking accommodation in almost every area. It's worth joining them anyway to keep an eye on what is available – but very frequently you will also find warnings about scammers or bad landlords. Do try not to get drawn into the dramas that sometimes erupt on these pages (plenty of landlords are members), but you can often learn valuable details about an area through them. As always be cautious, as lots of those offering rooms on these Facebook groups are scammers themselves – it really is a nightmare, so haunt the groups for a while and watch closely to see what's happening. Think of yourself as a spy!

Packing up

Once you know for sure you will be moving, it's a good idea to start packing up your possessions, even if you don't have a definite date or place to move to. Packing always takes longer than you think, and it's surprising how much you can do in advance. It's also a good time to start getting rid of stuff you don't want or need, as getting rid of unloved and unneeded clutter saves time and money on moving day. If you are leaving another place you are renting, this is also when you should start cleaning: washing window frames, inside cupboards, etc. Getting a place clean takes longer than seems reasonable, and if you clean as you go, it's far easier to leave it immaculate when the time comes.

Packing tips and tricks

Pack things you won't need for a while in stout boxes. Books and ornaments are a good place to start, along with things like Christmas decorations (assuming you're unlikely to still be at your current place for Christmas). LABEL these boxes clearly. Once you have a definite place to live and a solid moving date, you can start packing everything else. The last things to pack are the items you will need on moving day – pants, socks, toothbrush, kettle, tea bags and a plate. Again – LABEL THEM CLEARLY. You can often get banana boxes from your nearest supermarket: they are free, very strong, and although there is a hole in the bottom, it is easily covered over. They have hand grips, too, and are big enough for many household items, yet small enough to be liftable if you fill them with books. For the first proper move I ever did, I filled a wooden tea

chest with books – three tea chests, actually – and then was very surprised when the removals men insisted that I unpacked them and put my books into smaller boxes, because they were too heavy to carry. Things like bedding and clothing pack very well into those big tartan laundry bags, which you can buy cheaply. Again – LABEL everything. A trick I find useful is to colour-code rooms – blue for the kitchen, yellow for the bedroom, etc – and then use a label in the corresponding colour on the boxes and bags for each room, so the removal people know what goes where without needing to ask you.

Organising transport

However you intend to move your stuff, organise that in advance. Book a removals firm, or a van, or enrol reliable friends. If you do involve friends, please check every now and then that they are still free and willing to help. Your move will not be at the forefront of their brain, and being let down at the last moment can be catastrophic.

I try to get a few days' overlap between one tenancy ending and the next starting, to make sure I have time to finish the cleaning of the old place, so that I get my deposit back. You may need to book a professional carpet cleaner, and please remember it is very often cheaper to repaint a white wall than it is to lose money from your deposit. Having an overlap also means that, if something goes wrong, it's not as stressful. It doesn't have to be a long period – you could get the keys to the new place on Friday and hand over the keys to the old place the next Monday, for example.

Moving in

Schedule of condition and inventory

As soon as you get the keys to your new place, if it is a rental, you should also get something called a schedule of condition, along with an inventory if it is furnished in any way. The schedule of condition is a record of the property when you move in, and it lists the condition of the walls, carpets, etc. The inventory, if attached, lists the contents – sofa, beds, etc – and should clearly state their condition. It should list everything that is in there, down to mugs in a cupboard.

Inspect and document everything!

Before you move anything in, READ EVERYTHING CLOSELY – mark any portion of the documentation you disagree with, and take pictures of everything! If there is furniture in there already, move it to check there isn't an undocumented stain on the carpet underneath. The photos showing the condition of the property and its contents should be clear, not fuzzy. If the inventory reads, for example, 'one double bed, Slumberland, clean condition', it's no good having a fuzzy picture. And it's definitely no good if the bed is actually a Hypnos and has a sagging mattress and obvious stains and marks on it – because you WILL be paying for a brand-new Slumberland out of your deposit. Speaking of deposits, they must, by law, be put into a registered deposit scheme, and you must be given details of this when you get your contract. If it is found your landlord has not used such a scheme, you can claim money back through the courts. If your land-lord tells the deposit scheme he wants to keep a chunk of your deposit at the end of your tenancy, you can con-test this with them – but, of course, you'll need proof, which is why those photos are essential, as they could save you thousands. Your landlord can also keep money to cover any outstanding unpaid bills, or damage to the property. They cannot keep money for what is referred to as 'fair wear and tear', although there is often a dispute about what this constitutes, which is another reason why having photos can really help.

If you skip this step, it's possible you will have to pay for damage that was done before you moved in. It's REALLY IMPORTANT. Email photos of any damage or discrepancies to your landlord or their agent, or both, upon moving in. This means you will have a dated record, so you can prove to the deposit scheme that, for example, the stair carpet was not new and clean when you moved in, but old and filthy, and then you won't have to pay for a new one. Make sure you save any emails in a specific folder to ensure you can find them later.

Useful first steps

Locate the essentials: water, gas and electricity shut-offs

Make sure you know where the water, gas and electricity can be shut off. The water is usually a stopcock under the sink, but not always. The electricity turns off at the fuse box, generally, and the gas is usually a red lever next to the gas meter, which is often in a box outside. Check that the stopcock works to shut off the water, and that the fuse box is safe.

Read and record utility meters

Make a note of the readings of both the gas and electric meters when you move in. If you aren't sure how to do this, just take a clear photo on your phone. You can then send this to the relevant companies to set up your account. I'm not giving instructions here as meters often look different. You might also have a smart meter with a consumer readout: these automatically send readings to the utility company. In this case, email them the photo the same day you move in, giving your name to ensure they switch accounts, so that you don't end up paying the bill for the people who lived in the house or flat before you.

Confirm utility providers

You should ask either the landlord or the property agents which companies are supplying the property's utilities, if that information has not been given to you already. This probably isn't necessary in an HMO, as utilities are usually included in the rent. On that subject, if you are in receipt of rent benefit and you live in an HMO, please be aware that the benefit will only cover the cost of the housing – even though the utilities are included in the price, the body paying your benefit will deduct what they believe to be the cost of utilities from that. As always, it's essential you check in advance.

First clean, anyone?

Once all this is done, you might like to clean – especially any spots where heavy furniture will sit – as the place will probably be chaos for several weeks after the move, so you may not be able to clean carefully for a while.

Moving on

What to do when it's your choice to move on

When it comes to leaving, it's hopefully because you *want* to move on – in which case, your contract will clearly state how much notice you must give. Please note, if you signed a contract for a year, and want to leave after two months, you are liable for the rent until the full twelve months of the contract is up. You might be lucky, of course, and find the landlord is confident of finding a new tenant quickly and so is happy to let you go, or you might find the tenant yourself and get the landlord to agree to them taking over the contract. However, if you just up and leave, it is very possible you will get a bill for a year's rent (and if you don't, and you had a guarantor, then they absolutely will).

So, whatever the circumstances, in this instance, you must give the landlord notice and, on the day you specify, you should hand back the keys to a spotlessly clean and empty property. After you both agree it's clean and agree any damages, then the landlord should give permission for the deposit holding company to return your deposit.

What to do when your landlord serves you an eviction notice

You may find yourself in a situation where moving on is not your choice, such as when your landlord wants you to leave. Once again, the notice period will be in your contract, and you absolutely MUST get valid notice. At the time of writing, Section 21 notices are still in force, which means that your landlord can just ask you to leave at any point after the fixed term of your tenancy is up. There is, however, a plan to remove this, so that tenants can only be evicted for concrete reasons. Please also be aware that you must have had sight of the energy performance certificate (EPC), the gas safety certificate (if applicable), and the Right to Rent paperwork, or they cannot serve notice. Assuming the notice is valid, there is a regulated process that must be followed.

Firstly, it's essential you keep paying rent – your landlord cannot kick you out without a court order, and to get that, your notice period must expire, at which point they can apply to the court. That is when you get a chance to plead your case, if you believe the notice is not legitimate or valid. I must stress that, unless you have found some-where else to live by this time, you need to turn up to the court hearing and plead your case – it's not guaranteed, but if the place is in good order, and you do not owe any rent, the judge might give you more time to hunt for a new home.

If you still don't leave, your landlord can apply to have you removed, which will involve bailiffs turning up and changing the locks.

Hopefully you will have found somewhere else to live long before all this happens – it's very stressful, but it is a defined process and it is regulated. Legally, you cannot just be kicked out of your flat at the will of a stroppy landlord.

To make sure you are clear about all of this, and to check you are abiding by the latest legislation, please either check the GOV.UK site or speak to Shelter – both will give up-to-date and accurate information.

With a bit of luck, though, everything will go swimmingly, and after a few moves you will become a pro at all this.

2

INSURANCE

Legal obligations as a tenant

If you are renting, you have legal obligations to your landlord, and to those around you, especially if you are in a house share. If you do not abide by these obligations, you can be evicted. Some of that obligation is monetary – if you destroy a housemate's expensive laptop by spilling a mug of tea over it, you are liable for the cost of replacing it. You will probably need insurance, because, apart from your legal obligation to be a good tenant and a good neighbour, that potential financial obligation is likely to be more than you can afford. After all, how many of us have a thousand pounds lying around spare? You are legally obliged to insure your car, and very often mortgage providers insist you have building insurance, but it's also becoming more normal for landlords to require renters' insurance. This can also be referred to as tenants' insurance.

An excess? Let me explain

Before I talk about different types of insurance, I had better explain what an 'excess' is, as you'll see it on virtually all insurance quotes. Put simply, it's an amount you, the policy holder, have to pay out of every claim – so, for example, my car insurance was £700 p.a. (per annum – Latin for 'per year') and I agreed to an excess of £200. This means that if I put in a claim for £1,000 because I had an accident, I would be responsible for £200 of that, and the insurance company would pay the remaining £800. You will notice that the higher the excess, the cheaper the quote is likely to be. One obvious reason for this is that it gets rid of small claims – no one bothers their insurance company for an amount under the excess, and it also saves them administration costs. It's tempting to always get insurance with a huge excess and pray you never need to claim, but I'd advise against this, as it's quite common to put in a claim and find the insurance will only pay some of it, but will still expect you to pay the excess. You might put in a claim of £2,000 for a new carpet, say, but then find that the insurers will only pay out £1,000, as the previous carpet was not new – but they still expect you to pay your excess of £200, leaving you in a bind.

Renter's insurance: do you need it?

Be realistic about what you are likely to be able to afford – it's usually easier to pay an extra £20 a month than it is to have to fork out £200 in a lump. Equally, you might prefer to set aside money in a savings account. If so, I'd double it up to be certain there was enough – and, most importantly, DO NOT TOUCH IT!!!

The details

It is a condition in some rental agreements to have insurance to cover the landlord's property – and so far

I haven't found it too expensive. I've never needed to claim on it, but it would cover damage to my house if I was liable – so, for example, if I let a bath overflow and ruin the ceiling and floor below it, I would be insured for the cost of the repairs. I think this sort of insurance is vital in a house share or an HMO. In a sole-occupant flat, it really depends on how well you think you can keep the place. But if, for example, you use candles or are somewhat absent-minded, it might be a smart move. Hopefully it will cover you if you drop a heated iron and burn a carpet, say – accidents happen, and carpets are expensive.

Contents insurance

Protecting your possessions

Contents insurance is exactly what it says on the tin: it insures the contents of the house. I've never bothered, as most of my stuff is second-hand, and a visit to the recycling centre and the Red Cross furniture shop will replace most of it for a nominal sum. If you live in a high-risk area, it might be wise to have it, however. Have a shop around first, and, before you sign up, read the documents VERY CAREFULLY so you know what is covered.

Reading the small print

If you live in an area that is prone to flooding, you may find insurers will not protect you against flood damage. Sometimes you can opt to have items such as cameras and phones insured while you are travelling, which might be useful if you travel a lot, but pointless if you don't. Some policies don't cover certain types of accidental damage. Please read the fine print with care – some insurance replaces things with new items, for example, so if your sofa is burned in a fire you can buy a very similar one brand new from the shops, while other policies take depreciation into account, so if your expensive sofa is several years old, they will only pay you the amount they decide it was worth at the point of loss. The last thing you need after a major catastrophe is to find out you aren't able to afford to replace most of your stuff. Have a look on Facebook Marketplace, Gumtree or in your local Red Cross furniture shop – that will give you an idea what your expensive sofa will be worth in five years . . .

It is also possible to be under-insured, which is when the insurance company decides you undervalued the contents of your house significantly at the point you took out the policy, and so will reduce your payout by that amount. For example, if I insure my contents for £50,000 and have a flood, I may claim for half of that insured amount, i.e.

£25,000, but if the insurance company decide that your contents were actually worth £100,000, the chances are they will only pay half of your claim, so £12,500. Not very helpful. So be realistic and check in advance.

You can insure virtually anything, for a price, but please remember: insurance companies are there to make a profit, so be realistic about what you insure. I have my iPhone insured as it is my livelihood, and if it was damaged or stolen I'd struggle to replace it. I haven't got my computer insured, as it's kept at home, we have a very low crime rate in our area, and there is both a dog and a large son in the house at all times. If I travelled with a laptop, I would probably make sure that was covered.

It's worth checking if your belongings are covered by other policies – some credit cards offer cheap insurance if you are travelling, so perhaps your laptop is best covered under that policy instead.

Taking sensible precautions to protect your belongings

I'm sure you have heard this many times before, but it really bears repeating: look after your stuff!

Leave expensive belongings out of sight – it takes a second to reach into a window and grab a laptop. Have a lanyard for your phone, and keep it in a waterproof case if you go hiking or dog-walking. If you need to open Google Maps for directions, then step back from the road and stand in a doorway with your back to the door so as to make a phone snatcher's life harder. While most people are lovely, thieves exist, so don't tempt them!!

Pet insurance: is it worth it?

Pet insurance can be very expensive. I have Hollie, my dog, insured for a fairly low sum, simply to ensure I can get her to the vet and then think about my options. I knew someone who had four dogs, and the insurance would have been several hundred a month, so rather than insure them, she transferred that sum into a bank account each month against future vet bills. If you are on a low income, it's well worth insuring your animals, as then you know you can access care if needed. Be aware, however, that the cheaper policies often won't cover pre-existing ailments. Mine will only cover any ailment once, for a year, and then, when it slips into the next year, it becomes a pre-existing condition and therefore is not covered. It's a chance I took, as I really didn't have the money for more comprehensive care. I've been extremely lucky, as it turns out Hollie does need regular medication for a back problem, but it's affordable. I also have a credit card I keep just about active enough to maintain a sensible credit limit, just in case.

Extended warranties: a smart investment or a waste?

If you buy an expensive item, such as a washing machine, you are often offered what is called an extended warranty. Firstly, these are optional, as they are a type of insurance offered by a third party. Whether or not you opt for the extended warranty, you still have your statutory rights, so if your machine is faulty, you are still entitled to a refund, or a repair – sometimes a replacement. Check the manufacturer's guarantee, too, as that is separate to an extended warranty. You may also already have cover on your contents insurance, if you have it, so you could end up paying more on a warranty than it would have cost you to just replace the item with something new.

I urge you to take a look at the GOV.UK website regarding all this too, as they cover most of the above – and, of course, it is regularly updated as and when laws change.

3

PAYING BILLS
AND LOOKING AFTER
YOUR MONEY

Household bills

If you've never done it before, overseeing household bills can be daunting! If you are living in an HMO, those bills will probably be included in your rent, but, if not, they can mount up fast. Especially if you haven't got much idea in advance what you should be paying.

It might be a good idea to ask an adult you know with a similar living situation how much they pay for their bills – in fact, ask several!

Bills you may have to pay include:

ELECTRICITY AND GAS – if you have it. Sometimes these are supplied by the same company, other times they're not. When you move in, you should be given details of who the supplier is – if not, ask. You can change that supplier as soon as you like. If you are utterly clueless about such stuff, it can be a good idea to have a pay-as-you-go system for gas and electricity. It can work out costing slightly more per unit (although, if you shop around, it doesn't have to), but until you have a grasp of how much this stuff costs, it stops you running up a huge bill you cannot pay. Please bear in mind that if you DO run up a massive bill you cannot pay, they will force a prepayment meter on you anyway and claim the debt back through that. With electricity, the most expensive thing you can use it for is heat – heat is usually measured in kilowatts, movement in watts – so any appliance that produces heat will cost a lot to run. This is a function of physics, and there is no avoiding it!!

COUNCIL TAX is mandatory (unless you're a full-time student) – there's no getting out of paying it and it's a serious bill that can land you in prison for non-payment. However, you can find out in advance how much it will be so you can factor it into your budget. I pay ours weekly. Phone your local council and they will help you set up a payment plan.

WATER – bills are usually calculated based on how much you use, and there should be a water meter fitted in the street outside, which is read periodically. Sometimes you'll have a different company billing you for sewage. I have this system, and it means the sewage company bill arrives several weeks later than the supply bill.

TELEPHONE AND BROADBAND – not everyone has a landline phone anymore. We do, because I need reliable broadband and the phone calls are free if they are under a minute. I also like it because, if I am talking to a tedious relative, I can browse my mobile while they talk! I think the ability to rely on 4G depends on where you live. As we are quite rural, it's not at all reliable here, hence the need for a broadband with WIFI.

There are plenty of other expenses involved in keeping a home going, but these are the main ones – life can be very uncomfortable if you can't pay them.

Minimising bills

So, what about reducing those utility bills? Firstly, it helps to have a rough idea how much you use of each utility, and then you can head off to a comparison website. I suggest you use more than one, because pretty much all are paid a commission by the utility companies, and not all of the smaller companies are listed on every site. Have a look around and see if it's worth switching – if it is, the process is generally easy and painless.

Once you have done that, look seriously at what you are using – hearing about girls having 'all day, everything' showers terrifies me, and I suspect they are not paying their own utility bills. For those of you who haven't heard of this, it's when people have a shower several hours long in which they wash, shave, exfoliate and burnish every inch of their body.

Showers are only cheaper than baths if they take under about ten minutes – and it's not just the electricity (or gas) cost, it's those precious litres of water! Each litre may only cost a fraction of a penny, but those fractions really add up fast in a power shower.

Next, do you need the heating on quite so high? Always wear a jumper and socks inside if it's cold, then set the thermostat lower. You're quite comfortable all summer at twenty degrees, so why set it at twenty-five in winter?

If you have free minutes on your phone, then use them – or if you don't use them, switch to a plan that is more tailored to your needs. For example, I switched free minutes for extra data.

Bank accounts

If you don't already have one, you'll need a bank account, and getting one is a surprisingly rigorous process so that criminals can't use fake accounts to launder money. But if you are who you say you are, it's perfectly doable.

There are various types of accounts, but for now let's just cover the basics. You need either a current account or a basic account. Both allow you to send and receive money, to pay bills and to set up direct debits.

A basic bank account is for those with either a low income or a poor credit history – they tend not to allow you to go overdrawn, and some other services are also not permitted, but they are often a good choice if you are bad at managing your money. They will allow you online access just the same as a standard current account, and some make it very easy to track your spending, which is always a good thing.

You can usually open one online, or in person at the bank itself. You will need proof of your identity – ideally a passport or driving licence – and proof of your address – a recent bill, for example. Different banks have different requirements, and, at times, I have had to take reams of paper to my local branch to comply with their requirements. They will usually accept a letter from a GP, a social worker or probation officer, but be aware there can be a charge for this. Some people can find acquiring the necessary documentation hard. Speak to Citizens Advice if this proves to be the case for you, as they are often very helpful.

Please be aware that you cannot open a UK bank account if you do not have leave to remain in the UK. If this is a problem, there is advice on the GOV.UK website, or you can speak to either Citizens Advice or your immigration advisor, if you have one.

There are plenty of online banks and apps today that can help you to budget sensibly, but they only work if you use them as intended. You need to understand what you are doing – and work with your own attitude to money as well.

The costs involved with banking

You may be unfamiliar with the term 'interest'. Interest is the cost of borrowing money – money is a product, you can borrow it for a cost, and you can also lend it and charge money for that. Interest rates (the costs involved in borrowing) are controlled by the Bank of England – and they are well regulated. You may have heard of payday loans. These are sums of cash almost anyone can borrow, but, strictly speaking, they are designed to tide you over for a short time until you are paid. They are dangerously expensive. Interest is quoted as APR (Annual Percentage Rate), which is the amount you will be charged if you borrow money for a year. It's expressed as a percentage, so if I borrowed £100 from the bank for a year, at 33% APR, I would have to pay back £133 by the end of the year. It gets more complicated, however, because when you borrow money, you are often expected to pay it back in instalments – so that £100 might have to be paid back in regular instalments over twelve months, meaning every month I would pay a twelfth of the amount I'd borrowed, plus an extra 33%, plus any fees involved, and every month the remaining balance would reduce slightly. I expect your head hurts slightly trying to take all this on board, but try not to worry too much, as the take-away from this is that APR is a way to compare borrowing.

A payday loan, for example, might have an APR of 1,500% (you're only supposed to borrow money for a few weeks at most), whereas a loan from your bank might have one of 15%, and your credit card might charge 30%. So, please – a payday loan is to be avoided like the plague. It really is for life-or-death emergencies only.

If you have savings, you can expect to have interest paid to you instead. Of course, it's nowhere near as much as the bank charges you to borrow money – like insurance companies, banks exist to make a profit.

Savings and pensions

Try to save a little money, as it's a useful cushion in an emergency. I realise this can seem an impossible task if you are only just scraping by, but even £50 can be a lifeline in an emergency. Some of the banking apps have a 'save the change' feature – every time you tap your card, it rounds up the debit amount to the nearest pound and moves the change to a savings account. As this amounts to a few pennies here and there, you barely notice, but it helps! If you have a more substantial amount to put aside, you can hunt for the best interest rates. I have a savings account I pay into every month by direct debit, and it gives me around 6% APR. I use this to squirrel away my tax!

It also pays to invest in a pension. When you are twenty, your retirement seems a long way away, but it catches up fast, and when you retire you will need money to live on. A pension is a highly regulated way of saving for your old age. By law, if you are over twenty-two and under sixty-seven, and are earning more than £10,000, your employer has to deduct money from your salary and put it into a pension scheme. You can opt out, but I strongly recommend you don't do that. Money is taken from your salary, but the company also has to contribute – and it takes a very long time to build a decent pension fund. We still have the state pension, which depends on your National Insurance contributions, but that isn't a huge amount and there is no guarantee that it will still be in existence by the time you retire. Schemes change all the time, so please (once again) go to the GOV.UK page and have a look!

Bank cards and credit cards

When you open your bank account, you will be given a debit card – it's got a small chip in it and you can use it to withdraw money from the ATM (the cash machine) and also to pay for things by tapping a terminal. You can use it to spend what is in your bank account, and if you have an overdraft (an amount the bank will allow you to spend over what you actually have), you can use that too (I strongly advise you not to, though). Each card has what is known as a PIN (personal identification number). This number is needed to withdraw money, and every few transactions you are also required to enter it before a payment can be authorised. This limits what a thief can access if they steal the card. I hope it goes without saying you should never let anyone else have your pin. DO NOT WRITE IT ON THE CARD!

The other sort of card you can have is a credit card – either from your bank or from another financial institution. You will be issued with a credit limit – an amount of money you are pre-authorised to borrow. Depending on how good your credit rating is, this can be from a few hundred pounds to many hundreds of thousands.

The idea is that you use your credit card to buy goods and, at the end of the month, you are expected to either pay back everything you have spent that month, which usually costs you nothing extra, or pay a percentage of that money, which means the rest rolls over into the next month, and incurs interest (money you give the bank for borrowing money).

Credit cards can be a great way to budget for larger purchases, but obviously the longer you owe the money for, the more interest you pay (see p. 34) and you MUST exercise self-control, as many, many clever people have got into thousands of pounds' worth of debt with credit cards.

The other thing to remember with credit cards is you must absolutely never use them to withdraw cash – you can technically do so, as it's a service they offer, but they charge you an absolute fortune for doing it. If you need a sum of cash, it's far better to approach your bank for either an overdraft or a loan.

Try to avoid using credit in general – yes, it's useful, and, yes, it helps you to build up a good credit history, in case you later need to buy a car or get a mortgage, but until you are utterly confident in money management, it can easily cause big problems later. A friend of mine recently took a sabbatical for a year, carefully budgeted and went on three holidays. Each holiday was affordable, and was budgeted for, but within nine months her credit cards were maxed out, and the repayments were then enough to put her income into deficit. She spent the remaining few months of her sabbatical eating cereal and being slightly miserable. She was, and remains, really quite good with money, but it's only too easy to slide into debt without realising, then struggle afterwards.

If you have credit card debt, it's worth seeing if you can transfer it to an account with lower interest, as there are quite a few accounts that offer interest-free deals for a year on balance transfers. Just be aware that banks only do this to attract custom, knowing damn well they'll make money off you later on. If the repayments are becoming a huge problem, you need to speak to the bank and make arrangements for an affordable repayment scheme. If you do this, be aware they will probably be unwilling to lend you money for a while, and will also notify the credit reference agencies so other lenders know you are having trouble. This sounds harsh, but the 2008 banking crash was caused by banks lending money to people who could not pay them back – then things snowballed and quite quickly the entire world was in a major financial crisis. Banks are a lot more cautious today than they were then.

Keeping track of spending

In order to cover your bills and your living costs, it's really important you know both your income and your outgoings. So sit down with your bank statements and go through every transaction. This step is important, because all of us spend money we aren't really aware of – a meal deal here, a parking charge there – and it mounts up fast.

Now work out what expenses are unavoidable: rent, council tax, food, utilities. That list can be surprisingly long, and can often be trimmed back, but we will deal with that later.

Once you know what's coming in, and what must go out, you can carefully check though the rest. It's important to allow yourself some fun and pleasure in life, but the stress of being in debt can outweigh any pleasure in the long term, so get your finances under control early and then you can relax.

Student loans and grants

If you are a UK citizen and want to go to university, you will have to pay for it, and you may be able to borrow the amount needed from the government. There are various different types of loans, and the process is different in Scotland and Wales, so for up-to-date and accurate information, go the to the GOV.UK site and type 'student loans' into the search bar. Student loans start accruing interest from the moment you take them out, and then, once you have a job and are earning over a certain amount, you are expected to start repaying the loan. Depending on when you took out the loan, any outstanding balance is written off either when you reach sixty-five years of age, or twenty-five years after you received the loan. It is a huge sum of money for many people, and when you get your first job and are struggling with rent and expenses, it can seem deeply unfair that you have to start paying it back. I agree – but knowing what you are in for, budgeting accordingly and trying to make sure your degree is useful will all go a long way. Not all degrees are vocational, and that's not necessarily a problem – employers frequently require a degree simply to show a candidate is capable of a certain level of thought and self-motivation. Don't waste the money, though – study, do the best you can to nail a pass, and, once you have it, use that qualification as best you can.

When I was at an age when my friends all trotted off to uni, it was common to get a grant – a cash sum designed to cover the cost of living for less affluent students. Unlike today's loans, this did not have to be repaid. It was also common for students to spend the entire grant in the first few weeks of term, largely because, for many of them, it was the first time they had had access to a larger sum of money with no supervision. University bars were really cheap, and it's difficult to make sound financial decisions when you're so drunk you can't remember your own name. It was all fun and games until they could no longer buy food or pay rent, so had to get work at a pub or similar to make ends meet – and studying for a full-time degree while working thirty-five hours a week is both difficult and exhausting. I suspect this sort of thing still happens – so be aware of the pitfalls in advance!

Debt

If you are in a lot of debt, you can contact StepChange Debt Charity to get advice and help – I strongly recommend you do this, because you cannot ignore debt for ever. It will always catch up with you eventually.

If you are being chased by an agency for a sum that's a bit more than you can pay, but not enough to go into an Individual Voluntary Arrangement (IVA) over, there are a few things to note. The first is that once a debt has gone to court, and they have found you liable, it will haunt you for ever, as it is not statute-barred and will affect your credit record for years. The other is that these debt agencies have frequently bought debts. Basically, this is when certain companies (such as a mobile phone company) may have a lot of debts they have been unable to collect, meaning they may be owed, say, £100,000 altogether. They don't want to write that off, as it's a lot of money, but it's not worth their time to chase every debt individually, so they sell the debts to a specialist company for a much lower sum – for example, they might agree to sell it for 30p for every £1 of debt, as that allows room for profit for the debt collection company if they reclaim the full amount. The debt-collection company then offer you, the debtor, a deal – perhaps you owe £100, and they will write to offer a full settlement for £70.

This means you can negotiate. Offer them less than the bill in 'full and final settlement' (that phrase is important, and you want it in writing somewhere, to be sure that's the end of it), and as long as they make a bit of money, they are often happy.

Now to explain what statute barring is. It's the time limit after which a debt cannot be enforced. In England, Wales and Northern Ireland, a debt is statute-barred after six years; in Scotland, this happens after five years. This does not mean you no longer owe the money, it simply means the creditor (the person to whom you owe it) cannot chase you for it. There are three conditions to this.

A debt can become statute-barred if the creditor hasn't taken action to recover it within the time limit; the debtor (that's you) has not made any payments or communicated with the creditor; and the debtor has not been found liable for the debt at County Court. The debt may still appear in a credit reference file, which can make it difficult to get credit, and also to do things like rent a flat.

Managing your money

Now back to the management of money, to hopefully avoid you getting into debt in the first place! You are aiming to ensure you earn more than you spend – preferably with a few pounds left over every month to put in a savings account for either a holiday or an emergency.

You now need to look very carefully at where your money is going – and very often you will realise you are wasting an awful lot on things that don't make your life any better at all.

List everything by category – the categories are largely up to you – and hopefully you will quickly see a few patterns emerging. There will be things you buy for convenience, things you need, and things that you neither need nor enjoy. I once spent £30 on Sellotape in a month, because I kept leaving the roll where the dog could get at it, so I'd use an inch of tape, and then the roll was chewed up. I'm a lot more careful with rolls of tape now.

It's a lot easier to control your spending when you are aware of your spending patterns.

I find it easier to have two bank accounts – one into which my earnings are paid and from which bill payments are taken, and another one into which I transfer what's left over after essentials. I do not have a debit card for the first account, and I only access it on my computer, which stops me just transferring money out when I need a bit more for something else. This way, I ensure my bills are paid – even if I'm a bit short of funds and need to live on beans for the month, I will at least have light and heat.

Important: learn the difference between a need and a want

A concept you will really benefit from grasping early on is the difference between a need and a want – and advertisers have worked very hard indeed to blur the line between the two. Satisfying a few wants here and there is good for the soul, but buying everything you want just because you can is not. It devalues the things you buy, clutters up the environment – both your immediate one, and the planet – and makes you poorer.

Tying very neatly into that is the concept of 'enough' – knowing when you have had enough. Buying too much food, eating until you feel ill – we know these things do not make life better, but do we recognise when we have enough clothes? Or pairs of shoes, or – at the extreme end – boats, or private aeroplanes? Recognising when you have enough, and being satisfied with having enough, is a great blessing in life – it allows us to be happy and content. You aren't constantly craving more, and you don't keep feeding a hunger that never ends. The happiest people I know all have enough – and don't spend their energy chasing more. It doesn't matter what other people have, life is not a competition.

The modern world is designed to make it easy for us to spend money, in order to drive the economy and keep businesses afloat. Credit can be easy to get cheaply, but has a nasty habit of very suddenly becoming more expensive. The current cost-of-living crisis shows how suddenly things can change, with people struggling to afford the very basics. You cannot control the world's economy, but by being alert to the issues, you can insulate yourself somewhat. I will probably end up repeating certain things throughout this book, but they bear repeating: we

are trained from childhood to consume, and that consumption is ruining the world. Fast fashion is literally
drowning entire ecosystems – and draining your bank
account – one cheap jumper at a time. Polish up your
environmental halo and simply stop. Buy what you need,
and don't be seduced. Then you'll find you will have a little
more money for fun stuff: meals with friends, second-
hand books, and maybe even trips to the beach or to the
mountains.

4

HOW TO KEEP YOUR HOME CLEAN AND TIDY

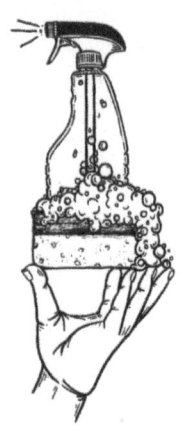

I'm not going to rehash my first book, *How to Clean Everything*, here – for a start, it's a whole book and far too long! But I do think it is important to explain the basics. Your home should be clean and hygienic enough for you to live a comfortable life. You certainly don't need to live in a spotless house, although I know some people enjoy that. It is very stressful trying to live your life according to what you see on Instagram, but it is equally stressful living in a complete mess.

It is vital you find a home for everything, as mess breeds mess if you do not keep on top of it. Try to put things tidily into sensible places so you can find them when you need them. I don't have an airing cupboard, for example, so my spare bedding lives under my bed in some of those lidded plastic storage tubs.

So much of this work is boring – some people put on energetic music, others podcasts, but my preference is for audiobooks, which I borrow free from the library. I have even been known to carry on cleaning for an extra half-hour just to find out whodunnit.

Once things are neatly put away, you then need to keep them in place – never put things down for later, put them away. Spend a few minutes before you leave a room setting it to rights – take dirty glasses to the kitchen, put grubby clothes in the linen bin, hang your towels neatly to air.

Try to do a few jobs every day – get into a routine. I usually straighten the kitchen first thing while I wait for the kettle to boil for my morning coffee, then set the dishwasher to run. When I come back down later, I empty the dishwasher while my toast is in the toaster. Do your laundry one day – and perhaps tidy your sleeping area on the same day, dusting and vacuuming before you put on clean sheets and put clothes away. I understand that, for those of you who are neurodivergent, this can be difficult. I personally find it easiest to do a lot of this as soon as I get home – even if I am tired, I still have momentum. Once I've sat down, it's too much effort to get up again. So, as soon as I walk in the door, I do that day's chores while the food cooks – then I can sit down and relax.

Clean the kitchen sink and the countertop every day – always wipe down after use and leave the cloth hanging to air.

The bathroom probably needs cleaning at least weekly, but this depends how much use it gets – when my children were small, I cleaned the loo daily, and genuinely considered removing the sink and just hosing them down outside as they made such a mess.

If you go shopping on a particular day, then take time before you go to clean and tidy the kitchen – go through your fridge to get rid of food that needs throwing out, and have a pencil handy to make a note of what you need to buy (and what you already have), then empty the bins, and wipe out the breadbin and food shelves, so that when you get home laden with food, it's easy and quick to put away.

As a lifelong early bird, can I request that the night owls among you do NOT run the washing machine or use a vacuum cleaner at midnight – it's a fast way to make your neighbours hate you. Generally speaking, it's unacceptable to make noise between 11pm and 7am, but I think it's polite to try to keep it down from around 9pm to around 8am – the dishwasher probably won't disturb people, and neither will a small handheld vacuum, but a large upright vacuum is another matter.

Things you may need

A decent vacuum cleaner is worth its weight in gold. If you are on a very tight budget, have a look at Facebook Marketplace – I have a second-hand Miele I bought for £40, and it's a far better machine than a cheap new one. Make sure you change bags if needed, and it's vital to keep the filters clean. A vacuum cleaner relies on the throughput of air, so blocked filters and an over-filled bag will affect its performance and put strain on the motor, thus shortening its life.

You'll need washing-up liquid, some cloths and a few stainless-steel scrubbies (found in the cleaning aisle, these are little balls of stainless-steel thread, and they are surprisingly soft and very useful for ground-in grub). Depending on whether you have hard or soft water, you might need limescale spray and anti-limescale loo cleaner. To find out if your water is hard, look in the kettle: if it's white and scaly, you have hard water; if it's clear of any deposit, it's soft. Alternatively, you can look it up on the water company's website. A squeegee is useful for all glass and tiles, as well as the bath and shower. I find an antibac spray is handy in the kitchen and the loo, but I usually refill empty squirty bottles with a little wash-ing-up liquid and water – I find it just as effective as the brand-name products.

As you go forward with learning how to keep your place nice, you may accumulate more cleaning stuff, but it's perfectly possible to keep a place clean and dust-free with no more than a cloth and hot soapy water. It's best to start with a minimum and buy more supplies if you need them.

Cleaning the house

If you live with others, be it housemates or family, I strongly suggest a cleaning roster of some description.

Work to people's strengths; there is no point asking a six-foot tall person with dyspraxia to empty the dishwasher, as your glasses will be no more within days. Likewise, expecting the person who never leaves their room except to cook to vacuum the living room will only leave you disappointed. This does need discussion, will probably involve compromise, and, to keep the sanity of all involved, will require clarity. It is obvious to me when I ask someone to clean the kitchen that I expect the dishwasher to be emptied and refilled, but sometimes I find the dirties neatly stacked instead. Bins are often a source of friction, and some people are happy to let them pile high rather than empty them once full. Clear communication is key.

Before we go further, I need to outline the process – the order in which to do things. Practically every cleaner in the country will do things in this order. If you do things in the right order, you will find it so much easier. You'll see results more quickly, and that will give you the motivation to carry on, even if you cannot do everything in the same session.

1. Get rid of rubbish: go round with a bin liner and collect every single scrap of rubbish. Then put the bag by the door in case you find more as you carry on. This instantly clears space and makes the place look better.

2. Then it's time for crockery and cutlery. Get it all up and out: load the dishwasher, wash up what can be done at once, and then the really crusty things can go in to soak. Do NOT do this in the sink, though, as if you run out of energy you'll have a sink of cold, scummy water, which you won't want to deal with – use a flexi tub or a washing-up bowl. Immediately, you'll find the place is looking and smelling more hygienic!

3. Laundry next: put what you can in the wash, then put worn but wearable stuff neatly folded in your bedroom, and the rest in a laundry bin.

4. Now we tidy. I suggest you do this with a damp cloth in hand to just wipe any surfaces as you go – but this is about replacing books on shelves, straightening and plumping sofa cushions, folding throws, etc.

5. Now you can see what you have to actually clean – start high and work down. Damp dust to avoid the dust returning. Vacuum everything! Do the floor last, working your way backwards out the door.

Room by room

The living room

Start in the living room. As per the master list, firstly get a bag and get rid of all the rubbish – leave the open bag by the door in case you find a few more bits while you are working. Then go round and gather up any cups, glasses and plates, and take them to the kitchen and stack them up ready to be washed. If you are lucky enough to have a dishwasher, put them straight into the machine, and if it's full, then turn it on and leave to run.

Next, if there is any dirty laundry in the living room, that all goes in your linen bin, and any used but rewearable clothes get folded up and put in your bedroom.

Now you want to tidy and dust at the same time, so get a cloth and a small bowl of warm, soapy water, dip your cloth in the water, wring it out as hard as possible until it is barely damp, and wipe all your surfaces. As your cloth picks up dirt, you can rinse it off in the bowl, before wringing out the cloth again and keeping going. As you go around putting things back where they belong, you wipe them off and wipe the surfaces they sit on. Once everything is tidy, go over the whole room with your damp cloth – and don't forget to wipe the edges of doors, plus the light switches. You are aiming to remove both dust and sticky marks and fingerprints, and if you do it regularly, things will look clean and shiny with very little effort.

Once that's done, you vacuum – don't forget to get into the corners and behind things. As well as the floor, look up at the ceiling and vacuum down any cobwebs you see.

The bedroom

Your bedroom involves much the same process – there will be more putting away of clothes, but otherwise the cleaning and tidying is the same. I suggest you change your bed linen once every week or so – it really depends how hot and sweaty you are. If you get really hot and thrash around all night, you'll need to change the linen weekly, but cold and tidy sleepers can get away with fortnightly. Definitely do it more than once a year!

A point here: if you want company in bed, you absolutely want clean bed linen. And decent pillows and duvets help no end – you want your bed to look inviting.

You also need a mattress protector. I cannot stress this one enough – accidents happen, and a mattress is expensive and hard to clean. A mattress protector, meanwhile, costs around £20 and can be washed and dried in a day.

The bathroom(s)

Bathrooms need a proper clean at least weekly, and a quick touch-up of the basin and the loo every few days. Before you do any wet cleaning, I suggest you vacuum carefully, as bathrooms are dusty places. After this, start with the loo: lift the lid of the loo and flush it, then generously squirt loo cleaner round the inside of the bowl, and leave that to sit while you clean the rest of the bathroom.

Move on to the sink and shower, using limescale spray if you have hard water. If you have soft water, a few drops of washing-up liquid is fine. Using a cloth or a sponge scrubby, work all over the basin and the shower in circular movements – you will feel the surface becoming clean under your hand. I keep old toothbrushes in my cleaning kit to get into corners and crevices. After everything's been scrubbed, rinse carefully and use the squeegee to get the shower and bath dry without leaving water marks. Don't forget to polish the taps and the outside of the shower screen – it makes a big difference if everything sparkles.

Now back to the loo. Spray the outside liberally with either antibac, or any soapy spray. Do the same for the seat – be generous. Let the spray run down and flush out the hinges, and get it into every nook and cranny. Before you wipe it off, use the loo brush to scrub the inside of the loo to remove any stains. Now, use loo roll to wipe all the exterior dry, paying special attention to the front of the loo, as there is almost always a grubby trickle there. As the loo roll gets soggy, chuck it into the loo and flush it away – no need for wipes!

On that subject, never put any kind of wipe down the loo. Not even the ones that claim to be flushable. Mostly they aren't, and unblocking a loo can be deeply unpleasant.

Never put the loo brush into the toilet bowl unless it is completely empty of anything except water. NEVER do this: trust me here. I keep a suitable plunger outside the back door in case of a blockage. They're inexpensive and well worth having for an emergency.

If any of you have hair longer than a few inches, make sure to clear the plugholes of hair weekly – it doesn't take long to completely block a drain with hair, and the chemical unblockers you can buy don't tend to dissolve hair very well either.

If the flow of water from your tap is either slow or rather splashy, it's worth investigating further. There is very often a plastic thingy, usually called an aerator, which is designed to direct and mix the flow from the tap – it's usually just at the end of the tap where the water comes out, and typically twists off for cleaning. If that's not the issue, find a small plastic bag, put a little limescale remover in it, and secure it over the end of the tap with an elastic band, then leave for several hours. Remove and agitate the end of the tap with a toothbrush while running the water.

A chrome towel rail comes up nicely with a spray of glass cleaner. I use hot soapy water and a squeegee for windows and mirrors (and tiles), but glass cleaner is really useful for getting marks and fingerprints off metal. It's great on stainless-steel appliances, too.

The kitchen

The kitchen needs daily attention. The sink needs to be clean, the countertops wiped down, and all food stored away carefully.

Your fridge needs cleaning out regularly – as discussed, the best time to do this is before you go shopping, as it's the perfect opportunity to go through the food in there and chuck anything past its best. See what needs replacing and do some meal planning. And, for the love of everything that is holy – CHECK what is in tubs – I left what I thought was a tub of Lurpak in the fridge for several weeks, but it was actually leftovers, so when

I opened it intending to butter my toast, I was greeted by the unholy stench of off cottage pie.

Wipe or wash the refrigerator shelves, and wash out the vegetable bin – I often put a few sheets of kitchen towel in the bottom of this to save needing to wash it out if a tomato decides to leak.

When cooking, wipe up spills as you go – and if you warm your plates prior to dishing up, the food will stay warm enough for you to rinse and stack everything else, meaning the after-meal clear up is far easier and therefore more likely to get done. NEVER go to bed or leave the house without leaving the kitchen clean and tidy, as food should always be put back in the fridge and surfaces wiped clean – if not, you will soon attract mice.

Empty the bin before it overflows – it takes seconds to pull the liner from a bin if it is not overflowing, but as soon as it is overly filled, you are likely to split the bag, drop tea bags on the floor, and generally create more mess.

Do not forget to take your toaster outside and bang out the crumbs on a regular basis – they are flammable and, even if they don't start a fire, they may well set off the smoke alarm.

It's well worth investing in a spatter guard for frying. This is a fine mesh screen you place on top of your frying pan that stops food spatter flying all over your hob while still allowing steam to escape. It also makes it less likely you will get little fat burns on your hands.

If you have a cooker hood, turn it on when you are cooking, and make sure the filters are clean – it really helps stop the kitchen walls getting greasy and stops the smell of fried food getting into other rooms, like the bedroom.

As a general rule, you do not want to turn your hob on full – food cooks better on a slightly lower heat. The exception to this is steaks, as you need the heat to sear them, but once seared on both sides, you reduce the heat and continue cooking them gently. Cooking over high heat risks food which is burnt on the outside and cold and raw in the middle.

Remember to wipe the fronts of cupboards and the fridge, and wipe the top edges of the doors, too – you'll be surprised how nasty they get. Use a toothbrush to clean the white seals on fridges and freezers.

The kitchen floor will need sweeping and mopping fairly regularly – again, bits of food left in a quiet, dark and unattended room are fair game for mice or cockroaches. A soft broom will gently collect fine particles into a pile.

Obviously you can vacuum, but I often find it easier to just sweep everything into a small heap and then vacuum up the heap.

When mopping, put HOT water in your bucket and a small amount of detergent (don't overdo the detergent, in case it leaves a slippery residue). Wring your mop out well and as soon as the water looks dirty, throw it down the loo (to save clogging the U-bend in your sink) and refill. You can get buckets that separate the dirty water from the clean, but I've never found them terribly effective, as they do not account for the dirt caught in the mop head. It's best to have several mopheads and wash them regularly – after all, you cannot clean with dirty equipment. Synthetic ones can go in the washing machine. I find cotton ones tend to tangle, so I tie their strands into four or five little pigtails first, and then I can machine-wash those too. Soaking mop heads in bleach doesn't get rid of the fine particles that hinder the absorption qualities of the fabric.

Two or three times a year, have a look through your cupboards to sort out the food, and make sure they are clean. Hopefully you don't open a new packet of anything before the previous one is finished, but it's easy to do – so check.

5

HOME MAINTENANCE ISSUES

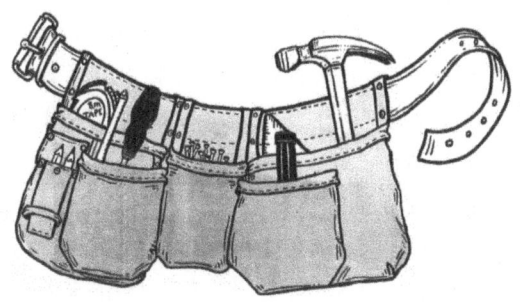

Blocked up? What to do when water won't budge

Always keep a plunger for unblocking the loo or your sink. Mine lives outside the back door. For the loo, you need to wait to check if the water is draining extremely slowly. Make a note of the water level, make sure no one uses the loo until further notice, then wait an hour.

If the water has dropped to normal levels, it's worth flushing again to see if that clears it – if the blockage is something like excess loo roll, it often just needs a flush or two to clear it. Just be careful not to have it overflow. Sometimes you can don a rubber glove, put your hand in, and pull the blockage free. This sort of thing can happen when an entire roll of loo paper has fallen in, for example.

If that doesn't help, then grab your plunger and carefully put it into the loo so the rubber sits on the sides of the bowl where the water normally sits, then push sharply down. Relax your grip and the rubber will come back up – push sharply again. What you are trying to do is force the blockage forwards to free itself. After two or three sharp shoves, lift the plunger slightly to see if the blockage clears – then flush again to check.

If not, then I'd advise calling a plumber. I don't advise using chemical unblockers, as they are rarely successful, and if you've filled your loo with caustic chemicals, it means a plumber won't be able to safely clear it. Also, it is entirely possible to blow up a loo if you inadvertently mix the wrong chemicals.

The most stubborn block I have ever had was caused by a bar of soap my toddler had dropped into the loo, so if you have small people in the house, be aware they adore putting things in the loo. Keep anything they could potentially flush out of reach, or have a bolt at the TOP of the door on the outside and keep it bolted when the bathroom isn't in use. Just remember that kids also love doing up bolts and keys – and you do not want to be locked inside your loo with a two-year-old rampaging around the house.

Blocked sinks? Firstly try pouring a kettle of boiling water into the plughole, as this often clears a slow-flowing sink. Then flush it with lots of hot water to rinse it all through – and then be more careful about putting grease and fat down the sink in future. If boiling water doesn't work, try the plunger. Carefully ensure it covers the plughole, then BLOCK THE OVERFLOW (I seal it with a strip of duct tape – it's easier than contorting my hands), before pumping the plunger up and down. Try this a few times. If that doesn't work, then you'll need to undo the U-bend. Grab a large bowl or, better still, a bucket, clear under the sink and put the bucket under the pipework. Use a jug to bail out as much water as you can from the sink and flush it down the loo. The next bit I will explain as best I can, but I'd suggest you also look at a video so you can visualise what I'm explaining.

Unscrew the U-bend, and all the water left in the sink will cascade into the bucket (hence why you bailed it out). Take the pipework and the bucket to ANOTHER SINK. Flush the water down the loo and have a look in the U-bend – hopefully you will have found the blockage and can hook it out and put it in the bin. Clean the pipe and, once it's all clean, reattach everything carefully and run the taps, leaving the bucket underneath while you do this, to check it's all tight and doesn't leak.

If the U-bend is clear when you check it, that means the block is further towards the drain – so you'll need to use something called a plumber's snake, which can be run down the pipe in order to see if you can fish the blockage out.

If that still doesn't fix things, it is possible you have a blockage in the drains outside, and you can clear that yourself with a set of drain rods. However, I'll assume you'd rather not, as it can be a touch grim. If you have rods and want to give it a go, then look up how to rod a drain online. It's not difficult, but you need a fairly strong stomach.

Gas problems: leaks and all the rest

If you smell gas, OPEN WINDOWS AND DOORS. Do NOT switch on the light. First check the hob or oven isn't on but not alight – strictly speaking, with modern appliances, this shouldn't happen, but things can malfunction. If that's not the cause, then turn the gas off at the mains – it's a red lever near the gas meter. Leave things to ventilate and then either phone a gas engineer, your landlord or, if the smell of gas persists, the gas emergency line. It is illegal to work on any gas appliance unless you are certified, so if your landlord turns up wielding a spanner, insist he contacts a certified gas engineer. Your landlord should also have the boiler serviced and should get a gas safety certificate every year – this is a legal requirement, so keep an eye on things and, if they haven't got a certificate, remind them it is a criminal offence not to have one. If they still fail to get one, then please report the matter to the Health and Safety Executive (HSE) using the LGSR1 form, which can be found online.

Electrical faults: how to stay safe

A modern fuse box no longer contains fuses which have to be replaced but a trip switch. If you have an older style box, with fuses, you absolutely need to have it replaced, as the new boxes are an order of magnitude safer. Inside your home, the electricity supply is divided into what is known as circuits. Usually the upstairs lights are one circuit, and the downstairs lights another. Then the sockets are divided into upstairs and downstairs, with things that require more power, such as the shower or the boiler, on their own circuit. Each circuit has a fuse (a trip switch today) and, if you open the fuse box, you will see numerous little switches. Hopefully they will be carefully labelled, so you know what they control. If all the electric goes off, have a look to see if anything has tripped, but quite often a complete lack of power to the whole house is a power cut rather than a fuse. If something has tripped, flip it back and see if it stays – very often it won't, and then you need to think about what the last thing that pulled power was. Did you just turn the iron on? Did the heating cut in? Whatever that was, turn it off and try again. Hopefully that's it, and then whatever it was either needs repair or replacement. It was the iron, though – it's always the iron.

If one thing just stops working, it may be the fuse inside the plug. This is quick and easy to replace. Just unscrew the back of the plug and you can prise out the fuse. The trick here is to make sure you use a known good fuse – for brown 13-amp fuses, that's easy, as you can just take one from a lamp that still turns on. However, it's also important to use the correct fuse for the appliance. The point of having a fuse is to protect the appliance from damage, and lower-power things such as computers and games consoles often have 3- or 5-amp fuses. If you use a 13-amp fuse on a 3-amp item and there is a power surge, you will fry the item. Get around this by keeping new fuses in their packets, and if you take a fuse out of a plug, then put it straight in the bin so you don't mix up new and old fuses. Reassemble the plug before you plug it in to test.

If that doesn't work, then take the device to be repaired. Sadly many modern appliances are not designed to be repaired, so you might struggle with this. Ask around locally (at the library, for example, if you still have one). We have a repair café near us that runs once a month in our community hall, and they will look at anything to see if it's repairable or not, so always check before you bin something.

And please don't mess around with electrics. People die in electrical accidents a lot less than they used to because of modern standards, and it would be a shame if you became the rarity who did. Experts are there for a reason.

Leaks: stop them before they wreak havoc

If water suddenly starts dripping from a ceiling (assuming you're not in a flat), the first thing to do is check it's not a bath overflowing (that can be quickly remedied), then turn off the water at the stopcock (remember I told you to check where it was?) and turn on upstairs taps. This is to limit the damage by emptying the system of water. If the water is dripping through the middle of a ceiling, get a bucket, place it under the drip, and VERY CAREFULLY make a small hole where the water is coming through. You do not want a build-up of water – the weight will bring the ceiling down, so it's far better to allow it to drain freely while you investigate the cause.

If the leak is directly under the bath, yet the bath is not overflowing, take the side panel off the bath and check it's not the overflow leaking! This is very common, as we all tend to put our feet up at the tap end of the bath and often the overflow gets dislodged.

If you live in a flat, then run upstairs and bang on their door; if you get no reply, phone the property manager on the emergency line. While you are waiting for help, start moving stuff out of the way – if it's a LOT of water, you might need to contact the fire brigade, but that's for a degree of flooding that is dangerous, not just a steady plumbing leak. You can sometimes turn off the water in the street outside, if you know which meter supplies which house.

The water meters and stop valves are outside and are usually under small covers marked 'W' or 'water' – there will be one for every property, so look for a smattering of covers up and down the street. You may need something called a valve key (you can buy these at a hardware shop), but many simply have a plastic bit attached – I have used a stout flat-blade screwdriver too. Open the cover – there is usually a polystyrene insulation cover, which can be lifted off – then turn the valve clockwise for off. Then replace the covers.

Please bear in mind it is illegal to turn off someone's water without very good reason indeed, so this really is a last resort.

Bleeding radiators

If you think your radiators aren't getting terribly hot, they may need bleeding. To check, wait until your heating has been running a while, then see if they are hot at the very top – if your rad is cool at the top but properly warm at the bottom, it needs bleeding. It's a simple job, but one that should be done when the system is not running – check online for step-by-step instructions.

Getting an expert in

Finding a plumber or an electrician can be as simple as phoning the first hit on Google, but that's often a bad idea, as you can end up with a cowboy who costs you a fortune. First of all, you need to be clear about what exactly you are looking for. Do you need a drain cleared, a dripping tap dealt with or a loo plumbed in? Trades-people have quite specialised skills, and you want to be sure that the person you are getting is trustworthy, affordable and honest – and can do the job properly. It's always a good idea to get personal recommendations. I find social media can be useful for this, as it identifies local tradespeople and allows you to check up on their standards. Ask around and find out what work they have done – and make sure you're not just reading a few reviews seeded onto their Facebook page by their mates. Pay when the job is finished, not before. Try to find out in advance roughly what the going rate for the job is, as this varies a lot by region, then ask them what they will charge. READ ANY SMALL PRINT. We had a drain clean-ing company near us that was featured on *Rogue Traders* numerous times. They always claimed to be a local family-run business, but traded all over the south of England. They'd quote a price that was reasonable, but when you read the small print (and it was very small print indeed), that price was for thirty minutes on site. Any time after that was charged by the half-hour, and the rate typically worked out at over £350 per hour, often with misleading and unnecessary work being done. People got presented with bills for thousands of pounds for jobs that should have cost a few hundred at the most. They employed large, menacing men, and terrified pensioners were driven to the cashpoint to withdraw the money – all because they had signed a contract.

When it comes to people who work inside your home, it's not only important that they be competent, but also that you are comfortable with them being in your house. This is especially true for people such as cleaners and carers – you must be able to relax, as these people will end up knowing a lot about you, so you need to feel you can trust them. It usually works best if you employ some-one who holds similar ideas to yours, as there's no point having a cleaner who insists on using a gallon of bleach a week if you are big on using eco-friendly bicarb. Once again, personal recommendations are best, as it's also easier to find out if they are bearable. I've had several clients who really weren't a good fit at all, and it's very uncomfortable for everyone. Check they will do what you need – some cleaners will do laundry for you, others will only clean. Some will tidy, others won't – and tidying takes time! Make sure you allow them enough time to do whatever you require. It's a pet peeve of mine hearing people complain that they've paid a cleaner and aren't satisfied with what has been done, but it's obvious they didn't allow enough time. Allow someone to see your house as it will be when they arrive, show them what you want done, then get them to say how long they will take. If you simply give them set hours, be aware those hours will limit what they can manage in that time.

Broadly speaking, I am a fan of community pages, but you simply need to be discerning as to how you use them. Lots of us have elderly parents who have a tendency to believe everything they read online, but I'm often amazed at how trusting people in general are – and scammers know this, and use the community pages to give themselves a veneer of respectability. Be cautious!

Fires and wood burners: how to stay safe and warm

Hopefully you have a carbon monoxide alarm already, but if not, please ensure you have one – they are essential for any gas appliance (which I expect you already know), but also if you have a fire or log burner – as carbon monoxide kills quickly and silently, and it has killed entire families before now. If you have an alarm, check it weekly.

It's also important to have your chimney, if you have one, swept regularly – once a year, if possible. Ours is normally done in late summer. Sweeps get very busy indeed as the weather cools and people start to think about lighting the fire. I try to get ahead by ordering logs and booking the sweep once nesting season is over. My chimney has a bird guard on, but birds nest in chimneys, and I prefer to wait until after nesting season just in case – that way I can be confident there isn't a nest up there when I light the first fire of the year, but also that I am not going to have to haul a baby jackdaw out of the ashes and return it to its furious parents (jackdaws are especially keen on a chimney as a nesting place). Chimney fires happen when the chimney is covered in soot and clinker – or when there is an abandoned nest inside, which can catch fire inside the chimney – and from there spread to the roof or a bedroom. Keep your fireplace clean, and if you have an open fire, NEVER leave it unattended without a spark guard over it. And if you have children, you need a fire guard that is firmly attached to the wall. Do NOT drape washing over this – washing needs to go on an airer placed far enough away that any spark will not land on it. The same goes for anything else potentially flammable.

Ash can remain red hot for well over a day, so if you are clearing ash, always use a metal bucket, and do not just tip the ash into a bin until you are sure it is cold. It's always a good idea to leave the ash bucket outside for several days before emptying it – and before it goes into a bin, please check it's cold all the way through!

Painting and decorating

The secret to good decorating is in the preparation – things must be clean before you paint them, stains covered with stain block, holes filled and sanded. There are numerous professional painters and decorators online to help guide you. Go steadily and (I cannot stress this enough) use dust sheets – cover your furniture and your carpets carefully. I always stand my tin of paint in either a cardboard box or a washing-up bowl to guard against spills. If you do spill or splash paint, then deal with it immediately – dried paint can be impossible to remove, but wet paint usually just requires perseverance.

Please be aware that some rental properties will not permit decoration, while others will insist the property is returned to its original state when you leave. See below for the warning about strong colours, if so . . .

Keep things out of reach of children – they love nothing more than painting each other, the cat or the carpet, and can do a lot of damage in the time it takes for you to have a wee.

Try not to be too influenced by fashion – all these black walls are very dramatic, but when fashions change and we all want white or cream walls again, they will need papering over. If you must have bright or strong colours, then hang lining paper first and paint that – in five years' time, you can strip it away and save yourself time and effort. The same goes for black woodwork – you won't always love it, and it will look tired and shabby in a few years, and it's difficult to strip. Be fashionable, but keep in mind how quickly fashion changes and try to keep the extreme trends to accessories, which are easy to change.

Gutters and roofs: home-maintenance musts

If you are a tenant, these are definitely your landlord's responsibility, but your guttering needs to be clear of moss and debris, while the downpipes must not be blocked. And your roof must be watertight – so keep an eye on things. Go outside when it's raining and look to see if your guttering overflows anywhere; if so, get it looked at. Unless you are completely confident on a high ladder, then get a professional in to do it. When it comes to roofs, look to see if any slates or tiles are missing or damaged. If so, they probably need replacing.

Damp? Causes and fixes

There are two sorts of damp – damp from the outside and damp from the inside. Damp from the outside indicates that the building needs attention. It's often caused by leaking gutters, leaking windows or eaves, or a damp course not working properly. Houses made from old soft brick can be horribly cold and damp if modern impermeable finishes have been put onto them – they need to breathe. If you rent, all of this is absolutely your landlord's problem. If you own your home, then speak to a builder, but make certain your builder has experience in the type of building you occupy – modern building techniques can cause long-term problems in old buildings. You cannot, for example, put a cement render on to a brick house built in 1850, or Sandtex paint on a cob cottage.

If you rent and you have damp, it is entirely possible your landlord will try to blame you and tell you to turn up the heating and ventilate more. Sometimes (but only sometimes) they will be right, because the other source of damp is water from the inside – if you take long, steamy showers and your bathroom is poorly ventilated (though that is a landlord problem, by the way), or you dry your washing inside, you are introducing moisture inside the house and, over time, it can build up. All houses need good ventilation, but in an old, draughty and expensive-to-heat home, we try to insulate ourselves as much as possible, which can mean that moisture hangs around. If you are drying washing inside, try to open the windows slightly, top and bottom – unless it is raining! Also, it's essential to open your windows wide every day, just for ten minutes, to push out the stale, damp air and replace it with fresh, hopefully drier air – although again, maybe not when it is pouring with rain.

I strongly suggest you buy an electric dehumidifier; they are expensive, but should last many years, and they are small and portable, so if you rent they are easy to take with you. I suggest a desiccant one, mostly because, in the UK, we need help in the winter. In summer, we open our windows and usually dry laundry outside. A desiccant dehumidifier blows out a steam of warm air and doubles as a heat source – I often have ours running on low just inside our bathroom, and it gets it lovely and warm, and is a lot cheaper than switching on the electric towel rail.

Once you have followed the advice above, you can confidently tell your landlord you have taken all appropriate steps, and if the damp problem persists, it is for them to sort it out, not you.

How to change a lightbulb: not as simple as it sounds

Once upon a time, this was simple – all bulbs were incandescent – but now we have a variety of bulbs. The first thing to remember is that lightbulbs are HOT, so never try to change one when it's switched on, as they heat up quickly.

The round ones that are set inside your ceiling are usually LEDS, but plenty of old-style halogen ones exist

– usually you have to pry away the metal surround and the light drops free, but some unclip, so you may have to look carefully. The bulb itself either twists slightly then drops free or is pulled out gently. Some units are designed with permanent bulbs, and when they fail, the entire unit has to be replaced. They were sold as never needing to be replaced, but of course they do – they just last much longer than replaceable bulbs.

Pendant light or lamps use bulbs that are either screw fittings (they unscrew to remove) or bayonet fittings (two small prongs which you push in and twist to remove). The central pendant light in a room is usually but not always a standard bayonet fitting. These two types of fitting are then divided into small or standard – in screw fittings, this is an E14 for a small screw and an E22 for a large screw.

Once you have the bulb out, you can note down the details (or just take the bulb with you if you are going to the shop) and buy one of exactly the same type.

Modern lightbulbs are rated in lumens rather than watts, to account for different energy uses in bulbs. Lumens tell you how much light the bulb emits, but they are also marked in kelvins, which gives the colour value – 2200 being a very warm yellow candlelight, and 4000 being a cool blue daylight colour. Make sure the replacement matches in every regard – unless, of course, you need a bulb that is brighter, dimmer or has a different colour temperature. Just be aware that, in the ceiling spotlights, an odd bulb will stand out badly.

6

HOW TO BUY, STORE AND COOK FOOD

Buying food well isn't as simple as it sounds – even if you have pots of money and go around the supermarket buying everything you think you'll want, I promise you will still want something else mid-week. Start by making a list: have a look at what you have in stock, as things like coffee and tea may not need buying every week. It's worth remembering that tea and coffee can lose flavour if kept too long. I don't advise you to buy the bargain pack of a thousand tea bags unless you are completely certain you can use them within a month or so – an unopened packet can last up to a year, but, once opened, that time is greatly reduced and depends on the conditions in your kitchen. Store cupboard ingredients are next – tins of beans or soup, stock cubes, pasta, etc (have your trusty damp cloth in your hand while you check them out and wipe the shelves as you go). Write down what you need to buy – and make a note of things you DON'T need as well, as it's easy to end up with a stockpile of carrot and coriander soup because you can't remember if you have any.

Go through the fridge and see what you have, and what needs using up, and then work out what you need to buy to complete a meal. Next, work out what meals you will eat for the coming week – allow yourself a little latitude here, but I promise you can save a fortune by not impulse-buying.

Buy smart

EAT BEFORE YOU GO SHOPPING! It's a mistake we have all made, but it can cost you £50 at the till if you are a bit peckish as you wander round. Don't forget to take your bags, either – I have a stash in the car, a stash in the shed, and, for emergencies, I've hidden some under the seats in my children's cars (shhh – don't tell them).

Despite temptation, don't buy reduced produce unless you can either use it or store it – a lot of food does freeze well, but you need a lot of freezer space to do this effectively, and not all of us have that.

Buy veg and fruit – you absolutely need to eat lots of it. Forget greens powders or expensive smoothies – just eat lots of fruit and veg. It doesn't need to be expensive: cabbage and satsumas are fine. And frozen is just as good if not better than fresh. The important thing is that you will feel much better if you get a decent intake. It's also cheap and filling – I find the very cheap frozen diced mixed veg and porridge oats make excellent padding in a cottage pie, for example. If at all possible, try to get lots of different colours – as much variety as you can afford. The humble carrot is a very affordable way to get extra nutrients. Don't neglect the cheap and cheerful stuff, as it's every bit as tasty and nutritious as the expensive varieties. Potatoes are an excellent source of protein, fibre and, as long as you eat the skin, vitamins. I would like to point out here that the term 'superfood' is what I tactfully refer to as 'marketing wank'.

I have a cold bag – it's supposed to be for picnics, but does an excellent job of keeping any frozen food frozen until I get home. It kept a shoulder of venison frozen solid until I got to North Wales once, and that's a five-hour drive! This is especially important if you're buying things like ice cream – in summer, I put a few bottles of frozen water into the cold bag before I leave home, so as to be certain I don't have to try to refreeze strawberry soup.

It pays to shop around a bit. I use one of the discount supermarkets for a lot of stuff, but I've found that their salad doesn't keep very well. I buy meat at my local butcher, as we eat very little meat (apart from any moral considerations, it's expensive), and he is quite happy to sell me small amounts if I want. He also has bones for stock, and the bacon is much better quality than the supermarket. But I must interject here – if you want to slash your food bills, give up meat entirely: vegans and vegetarians need to be a little more careful with their nutrients, but it's not difficult. Humans can be extremely healthy on vegan food, and you absolutely don't need the expensive meat substitutes. A variety of pulses (beans and lentils, for example) and grains should give you the protein you need, while seeds and nuts provide fats, and Marmite helps with the B-vitamins. Remember how healthy a tin of baked beans is: a slice of wholemeal bread slathered in butter with beans on top, followed by an orange is a delicious and healthy – and entirely vegetarian – meal. And in case you got caught up with ridiculous health claims online, seed oils are not bad for you, neither are carbohydrates, and you don't need to live exclusively on protein. No food is 'bad' – homemade pizza is delicious, and often cheap and filling. Eat as wide a variety of foods as you can afford, consume as much fruit and veg as possible, and try not to live on cake and chocolate, as it will make you feel sluggish. Humans are omnivorous – like pigs, we eat virtually everything that isn't poisonous – so don't get caught up in nonsense. It's all too easy to do, will cost you a small fortune, and could potentially make you unwell.

Shop seasonally: good for you and good for the planet

Don't be tempted to overbuy, and keep an eye on what's in season – food is often flown from far away to keep our shelves stocked with anything we might fancy, but that's no guarantee it's good. I eat large amounts of fruit throughout summer, but as the summer draws to an end in Europe, the fruit is flown in from further away and is nowhere near as nice. The exception to that is exotic fruits, but they still have a season, even if they aren't grown here, and are far nicer when in season. One of my absolute favourite fruits is the persimmon, and because it is only in the shops for around eight weeks a year, I never have a chance to get bored of it. Likewise apples: I do not think apples fare well when stored for all-year use, so I stick to English apples and rarely buy them much after January.

Street markets

Street markets can be a wonderful place to buy food, although I do find it needs to be eaten promptly. If you live in a larger town or city, you may have a reliable market that specialises in international foods, with delicious veg not used in traditional British cookery, but which is well worth buying. I always ask if I don't know what something is, or how to cook it, and there is usually an 'Ann' ready to educate me and make sure I am not fobbed off with bad veg. If in doubt: ask. Be polite and people are usually only too happy to help an idiot out.

Fruit and veg should look crisp and well coloured – if it looks limp and tired, it is not fresh. Beware of the cheap veg sold off at the end of the day. It is a fantastic bargain if you can cook it up that day (and possibly freeze it straight after), but be aware it is being sold cheaply because by the next day it will not be saleable.

Fish in particular should be firm, bright-eyed and NOT smell fishy, while the gills should be pink and the scales should gleam nicely. Meat should not be slimy or tacky to the touch: it should be firm and smell very slightly of meat. Do not be afraid to reject something. If you visit a butcher or a fishmonger at a market, you will usually point to something you want – a pork chop, say – they will confirm the one you've chosen and then it should be wrapped for you. If, when they pick one up, it doesn't look right, do not be afraid to ask for a better look and reject it if it isn't wholesome-looking.

I have a wheeled trolley I use for shopping. Although I recently learned to drive, I still find my trolley useful if I go into Salisbury market, as then I'm not limited by what I can comfortably wrestle back to the car park – and if I pass the cheese stall, I frequently buy more cheese than is practical (most of it freezes) to lug across town.

The cheese stalls in markets deserve a special mention here, as they sometimes have high-quality cheeses at very good prices that may have come from a supermarket after they have gone past the best-before date. Very often that means they are perfectly ripened, though not always.

This is because a supermarket wants a margin of error on its sell-by dates, and things like brie are frequently not properly ripe to the middle when they are removed from the shelf. I have often bought large wheels of brie for a fraction of the supermarket price, when they are at the peak of perfection. Once again, this does mean they won't keep terribly long, but most cheese freezes nicely. If not, perhaps you can cook with it? And, speaking from experience, it is far easier to eat a kilo of gorgonzola in one sitting than you might think. If you're interested, I had it on digestive biscuits and it was truly delicious. I regret nothing. In fact, since I first wrote that sentence, I have repeated the feat, as gorgonzola goes crumbly if frozen. But remember, sometimes the cheese may just be off. Treat this advice with discretion.

First things first: storing food

Frozen foods

Frozen food needs to go into the freezer as soon as you get home. I try to save space in the freezer by taking food out of its box, cutting off the cooking details and label, then decanting it into a freezer bag. Just remember to include the label you saved. I've just eaten some mozzarella bites I cooked thinking they were fish goujons. It was fine, but I doused them with tartare sauce and I'm not sure it was the best combination.

Fresh produce

After the frozen stuff has been put away, you move on to all the fridge things – keep uncooked meat at the bottom of the fridge to avoid contamination. I have a tray that sits on the shelf and, should a packet leak, it stops me getting meat juice on the lettuce in the salad drawer below.

The correct way to store food in the fridge is as follows: the top shelf is for things such as cold cooked meat and leftovers, the middle shelves are for dairy and cheeses, while the bottom shelf is for raw meat – but, as I mentioned, do contain it in case of leakage. Then salad and fruit go in the drawers at the bottom, with things like jam and ketchup in the door bins.

When my children were younger, I actually put raw meat in the salad drawer and fruit and veg on the bottom shelf, as we went through food quickly enough it was never a concern that the veg might go off, and I knew for sure the meat was safely contained at the bottom, but it did mean I had to carefully wash the drawer at least once a week. The fridge is coldest at the bottom, but the salad drawer is enclosed, as it's designed to keep the veg fresh, which does mean your nose may not pick up an off sausage if that's what you're keeping in there – so please check!

Cupboard ingredients

Once the cold food is dealt with, put away the cupboard ingredients. Some veg is fine stored outside the fridge – root vegetables are an example – but they need to be kept cool, dry and dark. I store mine in the shed for most of the year. In the summer months when the shed is too warm, I try to buy only what I can use within a few days, whereas a sack of potatoes will last from November until March if I ensure they are dry, cool and dark.

If potatoes are exposed to light, they turn green – avoid eating the green bits, as they will give you a tummy ache and if they get warm, they will sprout roots as they try to grow. If you have room, and time, you can plant a few sprouted potatoes in a dustbin or potato bag full of soil and, once the resulting plant has started to wither and die back, you should have a crop of potatoes for your efforts. Don't replant those potatoes, though, or they may well develop a scaly skin. As they are not a native crop, they are prone to viruses.

When Christmas veg is on offer, I stock up on parsnips, carrots and swedes, as they all keep very well in the shed.

If they start to look a little tired, I simply cook up a load together and then blend them for a vegetable soup.

Stack any tins neatly, and try to keep like with like, so you don't lose track of things. I decant things like rice and flour into large plastic screw-top containers, as the bags in which they are sold have a tendency to split and tear.

My containers are at least twenty years old: they were commercial containers of mayonnaise and mustard, from when I worked in a pub, and they seemed far too robust to simply throw away, so I took a load home and they have done sterling service ever since. They were free, and as far as I know they still make them, so it might be worth asking your local pub if they get them, and, if so, might you have some when they're done with them.

Spices

Ground spices do not keep, so unless you use a lot of them, don't buy huge bags – either buy very small amounts regularly or buy the whole spice, and use a pestle and mortar to grind as required. We have a local community shop that sells everything by weight, and you have to take your own containers. It means you can buy a single spoon of cumin powder, should you wish, and it's a big money-saver, as you buy what you need and no more. I just bought a spoonful of juniper berries for 16p.

Understanding 'use by' and 'best before' dates

Some foods have dates printed on them, but it hasn't always been so. There is a push at the moment to get rid of some of these dates, as people have lost the ability to judge food's freshness, and throw away perfectly good food simply because the date code has passed. Most goods are safe for some while after that date on the packet – there needs to be a margin of error because our supply chain is now quite long, and a few variations in temperature and conditions are allowed for. I have explained the two sorts of dates below.

Use-by dates: safety vs quality

Use by dates are connected to food safety: they indicate when food may no longer be safe to eat, and shops cannot legally sell food past its use-by date, but, in reality, it is very often perfectly safe for some time after. Cream, for example, smells and tastes unpleasant once it starts to turn, but I've frequently unsealed a pot of cream as much as a week after its use-by date and it's been fine. Learn to use your nose and taste buds as well as your eyes. Be cautious, of course, but just because something is out of date, it's not always necessary to throw it away – just have a look first. If you judge it to be okay, please ensure you cook it thoroughly, and if you think it tastes or smells strange, err on the side of safety.

Best-before dates: quality, not safety

Best-before dates relate to food quality: they simply indicate a point at which something may deteriorate. Salt, for example, may start to clump together and become lumpy, and the colour can fade or the texture may become altered. There are plenty of companies that specialise in selling goods that are close to or just past their best-before dates, and you can get some cracking bargains from them.

A word of warning – if a tin has started to swell up, it absolutely MUST be thrown away. The swelling is caused by gas forming inside the tin. Tinned fish was once known for developing botulism, which often proved lethal. There is even a Monty Python sketch that references this, as it was well known. To reassure you, our modern food standards mean this is now exceedingly rare, and the worst you are likely to get from a swollen can is bean juice exploding in your face if you try and open it. But I really must make it clear: please don't eat the contents.

Cooking

The importance of cooking

I'm not giving you a heap of recipes, but I reckon that if you understand what you are doing and why when you cook, it's easier to come up with edible food. Learning to cook is an essential skill, as it means you can control your food budget better, and eat a better diet by avoiding too much ultra-processed food.

Firstly, why do we cook in the first place?

There is a suggestion that the ability to cook food is what prompted us to develop our large brains, because cooking makes food easier to digest, and it allows us to get more calories. Cooking helps remove pathogens and some toxins, and it also alters taste and appearance, making a wider range of foods available to us.

Different cooking methods: wet, dry and fry

There are various ways of cooking. Wet cooking involves boiling or steaming food, either in water or some other liquid; dry cooking is something like roasting or grilling with direct heat; and then you can fry in fat or oil.

Microwaves work by exciting the water in food and then it self-heats, so microwaving is a form of wet cooking, as no dry heat is used.

Cooking proteins

When you cook protein slowly, you can get it to a point where it is just set and tender, or you can cook it fast at very high temperatures. But if we cook it at a high heat for longer, it can go hard and rubbery. For example, a chunk of meat thrown onto a flame cooks fast. Leave it too long, however, and it can become tough and chewy. If you cook the same piece of meat gently with liquid, it becomes tender and succulent. It's why we split meat into cuts suitable for roasting and cuts suitable for casseroles. Very often you combine the two methods. For example, you might heat a pan until it's really hot, add a piece of food, and let that blast of heat rapidly cook and brown the outside, leaving the inside raw. If you were to continue cooking it at a high temperature, the food would burn on the outside long before it was cooked in the middle, so we turn the heat down once it's browned to continue to cook gently and slowly, until the middle is cooked properly.

Wet cooking can be super fast if you steam under pressure, which you can do in pressure cookers or Instant Pot-style multicookers, but your food will not brown, so can look grey and unappealing. This is why we often sear meat in a hot pan before continuing to cook more slowly in liquid. Unless you are cooking under pressure, wet cooking is limited by the temperature at which water boils, so it's ideal for proteins that might become tough if cooked quickly at high heat.

Let's circle back to our chunk of meat. A tender cut comes from a part of the animal that hasn't done much work (remember that meat is muscle tissue), whereas other cuts, such as legs, do a lot of work, so end up quite tough. A steak is a tender cut, so it can be grilled hot and fast and remain chewable, but a cut from the leg cooked in the same way would be impossible to eat.

A tougher cut can be cooked slowly and gently to create a tender, succulent casserole. To start with, brown your chuck of meat in fat first to make it an attractive colour; this also gives you the benefit of the slight taste alteration that browning causes. Next, add your liquid – water will do, but won't taste as great as wine, stock or beer – and some other nice-tasting things: salt, pepper, some nice herbs, a few spices. Perhaps some vegetables would be good? Try adding some browned onions, some garlic, maybe a potato to thicken the liquid. Then cook it all gently for an hour or so, never letting the liquid boil. This will give you a tasty stew, and the variations are limited only by your imagination and what is actually nice to eat. Use a search engine to find good recipes, as stewing and braising are methods of cooking used the world over, so you will find thousands of variations.

Tender cuts of meat, meanwhile, need quicker methods. A steak, for example, is usually fried or grilled until brown on each side, and only just cooked in the middle. If you overcook it, then it becomes dry and rubbery, just as tougher meat does, and it often lacks the flavour to be cooked for longer. Fish is tender and delicate, so is fried or steamed for quite brief periods. Roasting is used for larger chunks of protein that will take longer to cook than is possible when frying, and we usually calculate how long a piece of meat needs based on its weight – once again, look online for the charts that tell you what's required. It is vital that some meats are cooked to a specific internal temperature, in order to kill bacteria and any internal parasites. In the UK, this advice is usually given in relation to chicken and pork, but please, as ever, check, as the advice changes over time. It's well worth buying a cooking thermometer for this purpose; they are cheap enough, as they are pretty much a metal skewer with a temperature gauge at one end. You stick it into the meat so the tip is in the centre of the thickest part, and then wait a few minutes to see how hot it is. Mine has saved me its cost many times over, and if you cook for the public, it is essential you know that things are properly cooked before they are served, so you can be certain all pathogens have been killed.

Cooking vegetables

Vegetables are a not dissimilar proposition. Generally speaking, root vegetables are quite fibrous, and made up of indigestible starch, which needs quite long cooking times in order to break down the starch and fibre, but things that grow above the ground can be cooked quickly. If you are boiling your veg, remember to only put the veg into the water when the water is at a rolling boil. The exception here is root veg, which can go into cold water. Once added, keep the heat high in order to bring the temperature back up quickly. Some things will be ready almost at once, while other slightly tougher veg will need a bit longer. Leafy veg is often best just rinsed under the tap, then shaken to leave just a little water clinging to it, before being put into a hot pan with a knob of butter and just moved around until it has wilted down into nothing. You may be surprised at how close to nothing that is: a huge bag of spinach feeds two as a modest side vegetable. Tougher stuff like kale and cabbage usually needs longer. If you experiment, you'll quickly gauge what's needed: vegetables that are tough and fibrous when raw will need cooking for longer than ones that are tender and crunchy. Most vegetables can be eaten raw, but not potatoes, parsnips (I think they are safe, they just don't taste great) or swede. Root vegetables are tough in general, so if you are eating them raw, try grating them. It's not necessarily better for you to eat things raw, though. If you cook things properly, you don't lose much in the way of nutrients, and as things are easier to digest when cooked, it ends up being mostly equal. Having said THAT, make sure you cook green veg properly – make sure it's clean, and roughly even in size, bring your water up to a rolling boil and plunge the veg in, keep the heat high to bring the water back up to the boil, then cook until tender enough for your liking (in most cases that is a matter of a few minutes). Leafy veg will need very little water, as it wilts and condenses in volume. Things such as broccoli or sprouts need plenty of water, however, so that the water doesn't cool down as much when you put the veg in, which in turn means the veg keeps its good colour.

Cooking legumes and carbohydrates

Most dried legumes – beans and peas, etc – need soaking for twenty-four hours before cooking. They absorb a large amount of water and roughly treble in size, so always ensure they are adequately covered with water or you'll come in from work expecting to be able to use the beans only to discover half of them haven't rehydrated. Please note that some dried pulses contain a toxin, which is neutralised by boiling rapidly for ten minutes, so when your beans are rehydrated, rinse them off and put them into a pan of water, then boil hard for ten minutes. After that, they can be cooked as you wish.

Rice and pasta also need more water than you think, and pasta requires a LOT of salt. The cooking water should be like sea water. If you don't salt the water properly, any sauce you put on the pasta will taste bland and unappetising. Well-cooked pasta is nice with just butter and pepper – if you are broke and starving hungry, that's well worth knowing. A little garlic or lemon juice also helps.

Potatoes also need very salty water when cooking, as the starch in them absorbs salt from the water. For perfect roast potatoes, peel and cut the spuds to size, put them in cold water with a lot of salt, then bring them to the boil. Boil for two or three minutes before draining. Once drained, shake hard in the pot with the lid on to fluff the outside. Then roast in hot fat for an hour. The heavily salted water ensures the insides taste good.

Cooking sauce and gravy

Sauces and gravies add both moisture and flavour to the food with which they are served, so gravies are often made with the water from cooking your veg, with the addition of any meat juice from the pan. Even the humble gravy granule is improved if made up with vegetable water. If you have made a roast, try making the gravy in the roasting tin after you have removed the meat and any veg you cooked in it, as all those little brown bits are full of flavour. If you don't like granules (I'm not a fan), then learn how to make a basic roux with flour. Simply heat oil or fat in a pan then add an equal volume of flour. Cook for a moment or so, then slowly stir in some of your liquid. Take the pan off the heat and keep adding the liquid a little at a time, stirring to avoid lumps. Once you've got the lumps out, return the pan to the heat, stirring constantly, and bring it back up to the boil. Add more liquid as you go to get the consistency you desire. Remember:

you can always add more liquid, but, once it's in, you cannot get it out.

For a semi-thick consistency, use around 30g each of flour and fat, then add around 250–300ml of your liquid. For gravy, that liquid would be meat juice and veg water, while for cheese sauce it would be milk. Add seasoning, and anything else you desire. If you want your sauce thicker, use less liquid: if it's too thick, add more – just go slowly and keep beating to avoid lumps! For reference, a pint of gravy or sauce is roughly enough for four people – depending on the people, of course. I can manage a pint of bread sauce to myself!

What to do with leftovers? Make soup

Soups are essentially a liquidised meal – if you have a blender, you can make soup. No need for a recipe. I have made leftover roast dinner soup many times: everything but the meat and Yorkshire pudding is blended until smooth. I then add stock of a matching flavour until it is soupy in consistency, before adding the leftover meat, finely chopped, and reheating it. Hundreds of recipe ideas can be found online – use them as a guide only, though, as neither soup nor stew need to be very precise.

One point worth noting is that a tired bag of salad that needs using up can be tipped into a soup and cooked. It's just a great way to avoid food waste: chop up all the veg that needs using, including salad, then simmer gently in stock or water until tender, before blending until it's as smooth or chunky as you prefer. Add seasoning and a splash of cream if you like it, and a warming soup is your reward.

The basics: pastry, cake and bread

Pastry, cake and bread essentially use the protein in flour to make different textures. Bread is made using what's known as strong flour, which contains far more protein. The flour is kneaded with water to make that protein link up into long, elastic strands, and then we use yeast to make the gas that raises it. This combination is put into a hot oven to both cook the dough and set that elastic, airy mass into shape. All that is needed to make bread is flour, water and yeast. We add other stuff to help with texture and taste, or to help it keep, but it's not, strictly speaking, necessary.

Pastry is made with soft flour (this has much less protein in it) combined with mostly fat and just a little water. You don't want that protein to link up too much, because it would make the pastry tough and hard to bite, so you gently rub the fat (any fat works, but usually butter and lard are used together) into the flour, using around half the weight of the flour in fat. To rub it in, you chop the fat into small bits, stir it through the flour and then, with clean hands, pinch a bit of the mix between your fingers and rub your fingertips together, letting the mixture fall as you do it. After a while the fat and flour are pushed together and the mixture looks like fine breadcrumbs. Add a little bit of cold water at this point and gently squeeze the mixture together into a ball before rolling out as needed.

Cake also uses soft flour to make the results crumbly and soft, but you add a raising agent – usually a commercial powder – along with eggs, sugar and – usually but not always – fat. You don't want your cake to be tough, or chewy like bread.

Cakes are far simpler than you would think – it takes precision and skill to bake a prize-winning cake, but the basic principles are simple. Flour, when heated with liquid, swells and bursts open, releasing starch, which is the same thing that happened when you made your roux (see p. 103). Keep cooking and use less liquid, so the starch goes rubbery. Add fat and sugar and the rubberiness becomes crumblier, and nicer, and the sugar makes it taste good. Eggs further enrich the mixture. You want some air bubbles in it, too, to stop it becoming a leaden lump – some of these bubbles comes from the mixing process, but for more of them we add raising agents. Raising agents give off gas (usually carbon dioxide) when mixed with liquid and heated.

For a simple cake, you need a bowl, a spatula or spoon (an electric beater makes life easier, but it's not essential), a cake tin and a set of kitchen scales. Weigh two or three eggs, then measure out the same weight of self-raising flour and butter (any fat will do, even lard, but butter or spread tastes best). Preheat your oven to 180–200°C, find a cake tin and, as you are new to this, cut a circle of greaseproof paper to lie flat in the bottom of the tin. Start with your butter and sugar in the bowl and stir them together – keep beating as hard and fast as you can, until it's all blended and soft, and has gone pale and fluffy looking. This takes some time and muscles, but persevere. It should be a pale, creamy-looking yellowy white. Then beat in the eggs, one at a time – don't worry if the mixture splits and looks odd, just keep going and it should come back together. If it doesn't, it's not the end of the world. If you want to add some vanilla flavouring, or some coffee, or even a few spoonfuls of cocoa powder, or some glacé cherries or sultanas, now is the time. When that is done, add your flour and GENTLY fold it in – use a table knife and make figure-of-eight motions through the mixture, lifting and folding carefully until it is roughly mixed through. The odd dusting of flour showing won't make much difference, but it should be mostly mixed in. Then put the mixture in the tin and place it in the oven for 20–25 minutes. Don't open the door until the middle has risen and the top is golden brown.

Experimenting in the kitchen

The above instructions are for a very basic cake – you can adjust the flavourings, and add more or less of each ingredient to achieve different textures, but that's the very beginning. Look online for different and more precise recipes and experiment. Just don't run before you can walk. It's not difficult to make a basic cake to eat right now (especially if it's hot, and served with custard), but a patisserie-level cake is a skill learned over years by masters at their trade, so don't be despondent if you fall short.

Throughout this section, you've seen me use words like 'roughly' and 'approximately', because the ratios of different ingredients change the texture and feel of the finished product. If you read a recipe book, you'll notice small variations in ingredients between different kinds of cake, or, equally, casserole. Those small variations can produce wildly different end products, so, as you start out, try to think about what you are doing and why you are doing it. After a very short time, you will get a grasp of how it all works.

Learning from mistakes

When things go wrong, don't panic – we all make mistakes, and learning to cook means you are learning how different foods behave, and how to combine different flavours. I was lucky, in that one of the ladies who brought me up was a cook all her life, so I learned by watching. I am really bad at curries and spiced food, though, as I've never seen it being done. I can cook basic, economic, traditional English food. If your parent or caregiver was from a different culinary tradition, your knowledge will be different, so go with what you know. There is no superiority in food. If you can nourish your body, and derive pleasure from doing that, at a cost you can afford, you are doing a good job. Food is, at its very heart, fuel for your body, so try to give it the best you can manage – it doesn't have to be gourmet, but, as far as possible, and as far as your circumstances allow, try to avoid too much ultra-processed food. Having said that, pizza is nice, and food is to be enjoyed, so don't get obsessed.

7

HEALTH

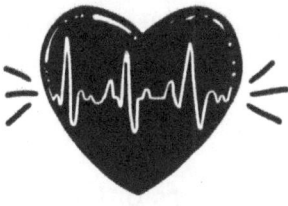

The truth about health: cutting through the hype and misinformation

This topic follows neatly on from the previous chapter. You see so much rubbish online about how to eat, what to do, things you must or must not do to be healthy, and the vast majority of it is from people trying to sell you something. A good lesson across the board here is to see what people offering advice are gaining from it – are they, for example, selling a course, or supplements, or a cream of some sort? For the record, this is a book, which will have cost someone money, but I don't sell courses or supplements. I'm selling advice. So burrow down into the health influencers you see online. Be it supplements, herbal medicine or a strange exercise programme, they are all selling you something! There are a few notable exceptions: those who stick carefully to the science, exhort people to be kind to themselves and do not try to push people into restrictive regimes and expensive purchases. Such purchases will not make you healthy; they will make you poor and possibly make you very ill.

The dangers of fad dieting

Fad diets have been around for ever. Obviously some people, such as those with coeliac disease and diabetes, have to be extremely careful about what they eat, but the idea that in order to be healthy you must eat a limited and restrictive diet is nonsense, unless there is a genuine medical reason for that restriction.

The water myth: stop stressing about it

Let's bust one annoying myth to show you how this starts, and how pernicious it is.

Water: most of us have been told that we need around seven glasses of water a day to be healthy. An entire industry has grown up around this fact. It's worth billions a year – and is based off a misunderstanding of human physiology. But you see this information quoted by what seem very reliable sources, so it must be true! Mustn't it?

We lose roughly 500–1,000 ml of water a day through natural processes, such as sweating, breathing and peeing. That volume is higher if you sweat a lot, or are in a hot climate, or if you are physically larger. All water, every single drop, is extracted from our food and drink by our intestines, whether it comes from a glass of water, a tuna casserole or a mug of tea. It then goes into our blood stream, and that increases our blood pressure a little and, at a certain point, forces open the nephrons in our kidneys. They act as filters for our blood, removing the waste products we don't want or need, before directing them as urine into our bladder, from whence they are ejected. Your kidneys filter somewhere in the region of 180 litres of blood every day, so trying to ensure at least three litres of that is plain water makes no difference at all to how well your kidneys work. Tea and coffee are just as useful as Evian.

If we intake enough water from ALL SOURCES to keep our blood at the correct dilution, we remain in balance. If we drink too much plain water or too little, we can throw that balance out of whack and make ourselves unwell. If you need more water, you become thirsty; if you are over-hydrated, you pee more. The best way to tell if you are taking in enough fluid? Look at the colour of your pee. It should be a pale yellow and not smell. Incidentally, if it's a red or green colour, it might be down to the food you've been eating – so don't panic immediately.

Obviously, companies selling bottles of water are quite keen on us clinging to the idea of drinking plain water, and if you like water, then go ahead. But don't stress about it. Drink what you enjoy and, as long as you're not thirsty, you are probably okay.

Now expand that idea outwards – anyone marketing any type of food will be extremely keen on pushing the marvellous properties of that food.

General

Food intolerances: find what works for you

Some people find certain foods disagree with them – I find cooked tomatoes tend to give me indigestion, for example, so I avoid them. Eat a wide variety of foods, and if you are vegan or vegetarian, you may wish to keep an eye on your intake of certain nutrients. Try to eat plenty of fruit and veg, as most people in the West don't have enough fibre in their diets. As I've mentioned before, frozen produce is fine (and often considerably cheaper than fresh). Enjoy your food – cake is delicious, but you can't live on it. Seed oils are fine. An all-meat diet is not healthy (and damn expensive too). Cereal and bread are fine. My only caveat is that a diet high in refined sugar and fat can often mean you aren't getting enough fibre or other nutrients, often because these foods satisfy your hunger quickly and so you don't end up eating enough veg and fibre.

Move

Get moving – however you can. We all have different bodies and abilities, and there are as many ways to be fit as there are bodies. Walk, flex, bend. I can't run, so I walk and cycle. Take the stairs rather than a lift, if you can manage it. Try to lift heavy things (lift from the legs, though – don't injure your back). We all know physical activity is good for us, but plenty of people are unable to be as active as they would like, so don't go judging others, as you have no idea about their lives. You don't have to go to a gym, or use expensive equipment – just use your body. Raise your heart rate a bit a few times a day. It's good for both mental and physical health.

Bone health

One of the most useful tips I know is about bone density. As we age, our bones can become fragile and prone to breaking. Firstly, we need to be sure we are getting enough calcium in our diets, but in order to keep those bones robust and solid, they also need a little stress. Weights will help with this, so carry your shopping, lift that heavy stuff, but also maybe jump down from the second step when you come down stairs! Little things can make big differences going forwards.

Teeth: the only set you get

Clean your teeth regularly. Teeth are expensive to fix, as there is nothing that can replace a tooth properly. Implants and bridges can cause pain and problems as they age, while dentures need care and upkeep. Veneers are simply cosmetic, and many people in recent years have flown abroad to get cheap veneers, which involves grinding away a large part of their natural tooth, only to bitterly regret their decision, as they are left unable to eat. Those veneers will need constant care, and they do not last a lifetime. But our own teeth, when well cared for, will see us into our dotage. Whenever possible, elect to spend money to keep your natural teeth in good shape, as no one looks good if they can barely chew.

Vaginas: self-cleaning, so no need for fancy products

If you possess a vagina, remember that it's self-cleaning. Keep your vulva clean with plain water, and ensure you know about condoms and are militant about using them! Cystitis and thrush are two common issues – and, in my experience, cystitis always rears its head at 7pm on a Friday when the pharmacy is closed. If it does, make sure you drink plenty, try to keep your pee as diluted as possible, and pee as often as you can. I've had some luck with a supplement called D-Mannose, but it's not a guaranteed cure, so the chances are you will need a short course of antibiotics. Try to access a walk-in clinic as soon as you can, as it's a miserable affliction and, if left untreated, it can work its way up to your kidneys.

When it comes to thrush, you can buy over-the-counter treatments, but, if possible, get in contact with your GP. Bacterial vaginosis is another nasty, and can be miserable for you, but for your GP it's just another affliction they can help with. I've heard of girls trying to douche (never douche – really, just don't) with things such as Dettol, and this risks making any infection FAR worse, by inflaming delicate tissue and upsetting a quite sensitive balance. NEVER DO THIS.

Sexual health

If you have the slightest suspicion you may have an STD, then go to the doctor, or to the sexual health clinic. It's confidential, and you should not feel embarrassment or shame, as it's the responsible adult thing to do. Any problem is always easier to deal with when caught early, and there's no need for you to suffer. If you have multiple partners, you might want to get checked over fairly regularly.

Check yourself – literally

If you own breasts or testicles, check for lumps and bumps, puckering or any abnormality – and if you find anything, get it checked out AT ONCE. Most lumps are totally benign, but for the rare one that isn't, you absolutely want it caught as early as possible. This is why screening programmes are so vital. If you are offered any type of screening please take it. I fully admit that a mammogram is uncomfortable at best, but dying of breast cancer is far worse.

Never be embarrassed to take a problem to your doctor. They honestly don't get bothered. They have seen more arseholes, for example, than you have seen Sunday dinners, and yours is nothing interesting or special.

The NHS: know how to use it

Now, the following is quite specific to the NHS in England, and I know it varies elsewhere, but bear with me.

The chances are that all of you are registered with a GP near where you live – most of us get registered as babies, and our parents or caregivers deal with things if the family moves. If your doctor is some distance from where you live or you simply don't know if you are registered or not, I advise you to find a GP practice near you and register. Firstly, it's free, and you don't need to provide proof of address, ID, immigration status or an NHS number. Have a look online, or just walk in to your nearest and ask if they are accepting patients. Once you've chosen a surgery, you need to fill in a registration form, either online (most GPs have a website) or on paper. They may need you to live within a certain distance from them, and it's possible they cannot take on new patients at that time, but if that is the case, they can often help you to find a surgery that will take you. You can register as a temporary patient for up to three months, and, no matter what, they can treat you for up to fourteen days, if necessary. So if you are on holiday, for example, you can usually get to see a doctor if it's needed, but they might direct you to either a walk-in clinic or urgent care, so be aware of this.

Once you are registered, please make sure you keep your details up to date, so they can contact you. This matters, as in England you need your GP to refer you to other, more specialised services, and you obviously want to make sure you get any emails or letters.

Getting an appointment – be prepared to wait

It can be difficult to get a face-to-face appointment. At the time of writing, my local GP has pushed a lot of appointments online, so do be aware of any issues, and please be aware that, in the UK, all medical services are triaged. That is why the receptionist needs a clue about what is wrong with you – it's not nosiness.

Triage is when things are sorted into order of urgency. It's why your wait at A&E can sometimes be many hours long, as they will always deal with life-threatening things before a cut finger. So while you may be referred to your consultant (specialist) for something, you will join the end of the queue unless you need more immediate attention. It's frustrating, I know, but you'd be angry if your father died of a major injury because the doctor was busy putting a bandage on a sprained wrist.

Teeth: dentistry in the UK

Getting a dentist on the NHS is rather like winning the lottery, as most dentists do not have a waiting list for NHS patients. If you are lucky enough to be registered, you absolutely need to keep that dentist, because if you lose them, you will probably have to go private. And be ready to travel if you need treatment. Even on the NHS, dentistry must usually be paid for, but it's far cheaper than private treatment, and some people are entitled to free treatment. Treatment is divided into three bands – A1, 2, and 3. If you go for a check-up, you will have to pay for that and, at that point, if you need any treatment, they will advise you what band you will be paying for. You only pay one band per course of treatment, even if you need a lot of work within that band – it's not cost per visit. So, if you need extractions, fillings and dentures, you will only pay one band for all of that, even if it takes multiple visits.

Be on time for appointments. I've heard of people being refused urgent treatment or getting taken off a register because they were a minute or two late. Most dentists are incredibly busy and, frankly, can make far more money with their private patients, so, as I said, be prepared to put yourself to a bit of trouble. At the time of writing, the maximum charge for NHS dental treatment in England is £326.70, but that same course of treatment can cost many thousands if done privately.

You can complain about an NHS dentist, of course. Firstly to the dental practice, and after that, if the matter is unresolved, to what's known as the Integrated Care Board. Dentists do have to abide by certain rules, but this is not much consolation if you have a terrible toothache and cannot get help.

If something goes wrong with dental work done by the NHS within twelve months, it should be covered by the NHS guarantee. That means you can go back and get it redone without an additional charge, but the catch is that it must be with the same dentist. Don't be afraid to go back to your dentist if something doesn't feel right or the work they did has chipped, cracked or broken.

It might be fixed or replaced for free. If the dentist is unhelpful, then you can take it further.

If you do have awful toothache, it's very likely they will give you a course of antibiotics at your first visit, then make a later appointment to deal with the cause. Please make sure you keep that appointment or the problem will come back. Your dentist cannot drill or extract an infected tooth, because they cannot numb an infected area, so you will need to return once the infection has cleared up.

A useful emergency tip to help with toothache is clove oil: just put some on a cotton ball and press it to the affected part. It tastes foul but has anaesthetic properties. Then phone 111, and they can usually book you into a dentist for emergency help. It may be a distance away, though – and, again, don't be late.

Basic first aid: how to handle the small stuff yourself

First aid for major injuries involves keeping someone alive until trained help arrives. Here I'm covering what to do for minor problems. Very often you can deal with minor illnesses and injuries without bothering the GP or A&E.

Coughs, colds and sore throats

These are mostly viral infections, and so they will go away on their own. There is no reason to contact your GP except in a few specific circumstances, which I will outline in a moment. Antibiotics will do nothing for viral ailments, but there are various over-the-counter medications to help ease symptoms. They certainly don't cure anything, but they make you feel better while your body does the hard work.

Firstly, take ibuprofen or paracetamol every four to six hours, and drink plenty of fluids. Sore throats can be helped by gargling with soluble aspirin – don't swallow the aspirin, just gargle and spit it out. Aspirin has a local anti-inflammatory action and can really help. Honey helps for a cough or sore throat, too – it's very soothing and helps with that nasty scratchy feeling. Inhaling steam, meanwhile, helps a blocked nose and eases a sore chest.

One of my favourite soothers is to chop a lemon, bash a chunk of ginger, smash up a head of garlic and add some honey. Cover all this with water and bring to a simmer. Make a big pan and keep a mug of the mixture to hand (rest assured, it mainly tastes of honey and lemon) and sip throughout the day. The steam really helps and it's a very comforting way to keep hydrated. Do the various ingredients help with seeing off the infection? Probably not, but it's soothing and might help a bit. Some people swear by it.

Be careful with paracetamol, as many over-the-counter cold remedies contain it, and if you also take it as a separate tablet, it's very easy to overdose. Paracetamol can kill if you take too much, so read what's in your medication. Pay attention to your pharmacist, please. They don't issue warnings because they want you to suffer; they're trying to keep you safe. You'll feel terrible for a few days, and you'll also be infectious, so please stay away from work and don't go around spreading it. Just stay home and nurse yourself. If you absolutely must go out, then PLEASE wear a mask to try to limit the spread.

The exceptions to just dealing with this at home are as follows: if you feel short of breath, have chest pain, or if you have a cold and you develop a very high temperature, your neck feels stiff, and you are sensitive to light; if symptoms have continued for more than three weeks and/or suddenly get worse; if you are immunocompromised – for example, you are undergoing chemo or receiving immune suppressant drugs. In these instances, speak to your GP. If your GP is not available, phone 111 and ask for advice.

Diarrhoea and vomiting (D&V) – hydration is key

D&V usually passes within around twenty-four hours. It's usually either a virus or a sign that you've eaten something bad. Keep hydrated, but squash or Dioralyte is better than plain water, as you will benefit from a little salt and sugar. Avoid fizzy drinks or juice, as they can make vomiting worse. If even fluids won't stay down, try tiny, tiny sips of water. Often you feel so ill because you are dehydrated. The winter sickness bug is known as norovirus, is incredibly contagious. Norovirus is something hospitals try to avoid, as any severe sickness can kill frail patients, so do them a favour and STAY HOME. If, after twenty-four hours, you are still vomiting, then contact 111 for advice, but usually at that point you will find you can tolerate a little more liquid, a little fat and small amounts of food. If you are still having diarrhoea after a week, call 111. Do not go out in public until the diarrhoea has stopped for forty-eight hours. All diarrhoea and vomiting bugs are really easy to catch, so please take precautions so that the rest of your household doesn't get it. Don't share towels or glasses, wash your hands properly, and spray the loo (make sure to include the handle) with a suitable biocide. I find bleach mixed with water in a spray bottle is cheap and effective, but you have to make a fresh batch each day, and, if it gets on clothes or towels, it will bleach the colour out. However, it kills viruses and bacteria. A teaspoon of bleach in a 500ml spray bottle topped up with water is adequate. Leave the solution to sit for a few minutes after spraying, then wipe dry – use loo roll for this and then you can just flush it.

Contact 111 or your doctor in the case of D&V in a child under one, or if you have blood in your stools or you are running a fever. Be careful with small children in general. Look at their pee; if it's dark or smelly, they may be dehydrated, and dehydration kills. So, once again, contact 111 if they cannot keep fluids down. If it's more that, or they are fussy and reluctant to drink, then try foods such as jelly and ice lollies to get that fluid in!

Minor burns and cuts

If you scald or burn yourself, quickly remove anything covering the burn, such as clothes or gloves (be careful if the burn is severe, as the skin may be damaged and you do not want to peel it off). Do NOT put any salve or ointment on the burn – just hold it under cool running water to take the heat out. This usually takes around 20 minutes, so keep going. Don't use ice or really cold water. Once cool, if necessary, you can cover it with a clean dressing. If the skin is broken, then unroll some clingfilm and cover the wound gently with that, while elevating the burn.

Most burns are small, and while painful, are safe to treat at home. Just keep the area clean and covered, and they'll heal in a week or so. A visit to A&E is a good idea if the burn is larger than the person's hand, is deep and looks white or charred, or if they look like they're in shock (this often involves cold and clammy skin, sweating, rapid breathing or dizziness). Take particular care if they are under ten, or have a medical condition or a weakened immune system.

If they have breathed in smoke or fumes, they may also need to be checked out – if possible, it's wise to drive someone to the hospital yourself, as it's very often quicker.

Chemical burns need to be flushed with cool water, so keep going. If this was a deliberate attack, phone 999 at once, but keep rinsing and flushing. Don't use cold water, but lukewarm or cool. In an emergency, speed matters, so bottled water is fine – just rinse that chemical away from the skin.

Minor cuts and scrapes just need to be cleaned and covered. Any little bits of gravel, say, usually dislodge when bathed. If, however, the wound is bleeding a lot, you need to put firm pressure on it, and elevate it to slow or stop the blood. In this case, if there is anything more deeply in the wound, do NOT remove it, but push down firmly on either side to push the edges together. Then go to either a minor injury unit or A&E.

Once the bleeding has stopped, have a brief look at the wound – larger deep cuts may need a Steri-Strip or to be glued together, so, again, off you go to the minor injury unit, but if it all looks clean and mostly together, you can cover it with a plaster, and it will heal on its own.

Be aware that heads and fingers bleed disproportionately to the rest of the body. A small cut on the scalp can look terrifying, and a very small amount of blood also goes a very long way indeed. Try not to panic. Just put some pressure on it and assess the situation in a few minutes once blood flow has slowed somewhat.

Something to remember is that the human body is pretty good at repairing itself, so, yes, while serious injury and infection does occur, most of the time when you feel ill, it's just a passing problem. Despite what Google often leads you to believe, most lumps are totally benign, most colds are just colds and will pass, and it's highly unlikely you are dying. Of course, 111 is helpful, but the call handlers are notoriously risk-averse and tend to send ambulances out even when there's a very small chance of risk, and obviously no one wants to overload the service. It can also take hours before an ambulance arrives, so let's keep them for things we believe to be life-threatening. If you can get someone to drive you to A&E, it's often faster. When you get there, you will be triaged and, if it's not urgent, you may have to wait, so try not to get cross. Just be thankful you aren't unwell enough to be rushed to the front of the queue. Equally, if something feels properly 'wrong', do push a little – my son collapsed his lung and, as it was chest pain, was blue-lighted into A&E, who were very dismissive, as he was not presenting with any symptoms that indicated a serious problem. His blood oxygen was good, his colour was good, he could breathe, and his heart was normal – but he had severe chest pain on one side. Luckily, we did push politely, and they did an X-ray, upon which they shot into VERY apologetic action and had him dealt with as a priority within minutes of the results.

Pregnancy – what to do next

If you have unprotected sex and are concerned about an unwanted pregnancy (accidents happen to the best of us!), then contact your GP the next day about the morning-after pill – they will prescribe it and it is currently free. You can buy it over the counter, but last time I checked it was £25, so while that's an option, it's cheaper to ask your doctor.

If you suspect you may be pregnant despite using contra-ception, or because you are hoping to get pregnant, then do a test. The cheap ones are fine. When I had teenagers, I bulk-bought them online for around 50p a test, and they work just as well as the expensive ones.

If you are pregnant, then you need to decide if you wish to continue with the pregnancy. If you decide this is not what you want, I urge you to get to your GP as soon as possible. No one will judge you; they will be kind and professional. Whatever you decide, they will keep it confidential, even if you are under sixteen. Please don't ignore it, because the sooner you decide, the better.

If you decide you do not wish to be pregnant, you can ask for the abortion pill, and at under ten weeks' gestation, you may be able to take this at home. You will experience some cramping and bleeding akin to a heavy period. You may also have to have a scan to make quite sure this will be safe, and you will be assessed. Generally speaking, in the UK an abortion can only be performed up to twenty-four weeks into the pregnancy. After this time, abortions are only permitted if the woman's life is at risk, or if there is a risk of foetal abnormality.

If you do wish to continue with the pregnancy, then, again, go to your GP, as they may examine you or do another test to confirm the pregnancy. Then they will explain how things will proceed. You will usually be offered an ultrasound scan to check everything is progressing normally, and you will be advised about your midwife and the antenatal care you can expect. At this point you will be given lots of information and, if you are concerned about anything, your midwife will try to help.

Please also know that, for numerous reasons, many pregnancies end of their own accord. Miscarriages are quite common, and this can be devastating if you were awaiting this child with joy. Please remember it's not your fault, and in most cases people go on to have healthy children. It's just that the human body is a complicated machine and sometimes things go wrong. I know many women who have lost a pregnancy and then gone on to have more children. And if it seems you have an issue, then, once again, your GP can direct you to the right help.

Alcohol and addiction: know your limits

Alcoholism and addiction are real problems and creep up softly. You rarely notice they are there until it's too late. You CAN get help, and you should get help. I'll give you some options later, but, honestly, it's a good idea to have enough sense to avoid the issues before they start.

If you are studying, it's almost a rite of passage to drink yourself to oblivion, but every year there are students who take that to extremes and then fail to get the marks they need. Further education is expensive, and generally considered to be an investment in your future, so if that is the case for you, don't waste the money.

University is not for everyone. I'd go as far as to say it's not for most people, so never feel inferior if you left school and went straight into a job. I did, as I wanted the money, but that comes with the same issues, as you can find yourself with adult money for the first time but no clue how to budget, meaning you spend your pay packet as soon as it comes in. In the days when a weekly envelope of cash was the normal way of paying people, there was the phenomenon of the Friday Night Millionaire: people going straight from work to the pub and blowing the lot in one night. Sadly, there will be many among you who had childhoods ruined by just that: a parent who kept their family in poverty while blowing their money on beers and drugs, leaving their children without the basics.

It still happens, so try to remember that while it's a great thing to go out and enjoy yourself, you also need to know when that enjoyment costs more than you can afford, not just in cash, but in relationships and lost opportunities.

Try to stop it becoming a problem before it starts – and, yes, we are back to understanding 'enough' again (see p. 46).

Mental health: just as important as your physical health

Mental health is often spoken of as a different category to physical health, but unless you keep your brain in a small onyx box, the two are inseparable. If you are not ashamed of having a cold or a broken leg, you should not feel a shred of shame about mental illness – it happens. It's not a moral failing but a physical one. It's normal to feel sad, or slightly 'meh' for a while; equally, it's normal to sometimes be elated and full of energy – but both states can become a problem. Likewise, repetitive thoughts or urges can come up for all of us, but and if these are causing problems either in your life or for other people, then they very definitely need addressing. It can be very difficult to have the insight to recognise your own problems, though, so if your friends or family suggest you may want to get checked out, it's worth speaking to your GP. Likewise, if you are concerned about a friend, suggest gently that a GP visit might be in order.

Mental health practitioners are often accused of just pushing pills. They're also accused of not helping enough. Mental issues are very difficult to treat, as symptoms are elusive and variable. An X-ray can quickly determine if a bone is broken, but there are no definitive tests for many psychiatric problems.

Medication

Let's bust a few myths here: pills are certainly over-prescribed, but that does not mean they are ineffective, depending on the person and the problem. Pills can be life-savers. Some psychiatric drugs have awful side effects and, in some cases, those effects are worse than the original problem, but it's worth trying a prescription for a month or so to find out how that medication suits you. These drugs do take some time to affect the system, and side effects do wear off in many cases. Some things (mild depression being one) may benefit more from lifestyle and dietary changes, so do try those first if you can. Sunlight (or daylight – we live in the Northern hemisphere, so don't get too excited), exercise and enough regular sleep are essential to human health. A varied diet with lots of veg, lots of colour and lots of pleasure is also helpful.

However, while the above may fend off a problem in the early stages, they will not and cannot help a seriously unwell person – depression, for example, is crippling. A serious bout needs proper medical help and, in these cases, medication is frequently transformative.

If you are in crisis and you are told a cup of tea and a bath might help then, yes, it can seem patronising and ineffective, but actually what you're being told to do is to try to calm your amygdala. Anyone who has spent time in hospital for psychiatric issues will have been taught about this. Although it sounds airy-fairy, it is the equivalent idea to resting, icing and elevating a sore ankle. Part of your limbic system is overactive, so, if you can self-soothe and calm it down, you may well avoid a nasty attack. Of course, it doesn't always work, but neither does ice on your ankle. It's worth learning and practising this technique, as it can stop people spiralling into a place they do not want to be.

If a friend is in distress, try to talk to them and calm them. Listen to the problem, and don't dismiss it even if it sounds ridiculous, as it is very real to them. You won't get anywhere by telling them they're being silly. Validating their fear, and offering simple ways to calm that fear, will be far more effective – and if you feel it's necessary, phone a doctor and ask for help. If you believe they are a danger to themselves or others, then try 111 first. If it's a real emergency, then 999 should be an option.

Most people in psychosis are only a danger to themselves, as they are in an alternative reality, and they may see and hear things which feel more real than you are. They are scared, deeply distressed and need calm help. But sometimes that means they must be taken to a place of safety where a doctor can help them. The police have powers to do just that. Having watched them do this, I can say they are generally kind and understanding.

8

HOW TO STAY ORGANISED

Life is easier if you can be organised, but that doesn't come naturally to millions of us. 'Life admin' can either be a constant struggle, draining your time and energy, or something that happens calmly in the background, leaving you free to enjoy things.

The one unquestionable benefit of the internet and smartphones is how much easier they make it to keep yourself organised, but you do need to take some time to set systems in place so the tech can do the hard work.

Don't rush this, as you want to get it perfectly tailored to your lifestyle.

Money – the foundation of organisation

Keeping your money organised is far easier than it used to be. You can get various bank accounts that make budgeting easier, and allow you more control over your finances. If you handle cash at all, you may want to make sure you can pay that cash into your account, and many high-street banks have closed branches. Some allow you to pay in and withdraw cash at a post office, and you can usually withdraw at any cash machine, but only deposit cash into a machine located within your bank. Most cash machines are free, but not all – look carefully. I might also advise against using run-down-looking machines, as I have lost money before to a machine that was not maintained and dispensed less than it registered. For this reason, I try to stick to machines outside a bank, as the chances are they are better looked after. As touched upon earlier (see p. 32), a bank account is essential for life today, and having a banking app on your phone really simplifies things. Have a good look at what accounts are available, and try to select one that suits you. Look at the features it offers, and any charges levied. If you are in the lucky position of being able to save money, then look at the interest offered on savings, the ease of access to your savings, and the amount you are allowed to deposit. Once you have a bank account, you can often open others. I have three – one with my original building society, which allowed me a basic account when I had no credit rating at all, another with a high-street bank I used to separate my finances from my partner's, and a more recent one I use for business. This system works well for me, but could easily be confusing for you, so think about what would serve you well.

Managing bills without the stress

Once you have tracked both your incomings and outgoings, as discussed earlier (see p. 39), you may find it easier to set up direct debits for regular bills, but make sure you have an online account so you get an email if the amount taken changes. The only slight issue with this is, if you are prone to overspending, you may find you forget to keep money in the account to cover a bill that's due later in the month. There are two ways to combat this. The first is to have two bank accounts – one into which your money is paid, and from which your direct debits are removed, then a second one that you use day to day. Never carry the card for your main account with you – just look at it every month after you get your money, then, leaving enough for all your direct debits and bills in the main account, transfer your spending money to your spending account.

The second is to ensure all your direct debits come out of your account the day after you get paid. Don't do it the same day, as in some cases they remove money several hours before deposits are made and your careful planning goes out the window.

Ideally, use both methods – that way, if you have a funny spell mid-month, you won't be able to spend the car insurance as it will already have been paid.

Once you know your bills are paid, you can relax knowing you have heating and lights for the month, along with a roof over your head.

Now let's sort out the rest!

Calendars – your secret weapon

Digital calendars

You need a calendar – I use the one on my phone. It snatches appointments from both text messages and emails automatically. Don't ask me how, it just does it.

However, I expect you can get that information if you look up your phone's operating system and apps. They do vary quite a lot and seem to change over time.

Alerts and daily checks

I set alerts for the vital stuff and have trained myself to look at the calendar every day before I get dressed. I just list every event as happening at 7am, then include the time of the event as part of the title, to avoid missing anything happening later in the day. Then, if an event has an alert, I enter it in duplicate at the correct time with another alert a sensible time in advance.

Want an alternative? How about a wall planner?

If you don't get on with your phone, I suggest a wall planner. You can buy one of these every year and stick it up where you can easily see it – on the fridge, on the front door or opposite the loo, if there is space. You write every appointment on it, along with the time and (if there is space) the reason for that appointment. My daughter colour-codes the items – red for important medical stuff, yellow for house-based appointments (things like the gas man or the plumber) and green for social events. But it's vital to keep these planners updated – make the entry immediately.

Annual admin and saving for the big bills

Things like car and home insurance are not things I allow to auto-renew. I always search for the best quote a month or so in advance, then wait until around a fort-night before the renewal date – if you get better quotes, then try phoning your existing insurer to see if they can beat that quote! Be sure to make a note every year of the NEXT year's renewal date, as it's easy to forget. My MOT and service get done at the same time, as well as my vehicle road tax. That gives me a hefty outlay at roughly the same time every year. Even if I pay the insurance and tax monthly (which, incidentally, costs more), there is always the risk the service will cost a bomb. I try to protect myself against this by putting £20 a month into a special account to cover it. I don't mentally classify this as a saving, but as a monthly payment.

Routines: find out what works for you

Talking of routines always gets me in trouble with the neurodivergent community, but one of the keys to managing life is to put systems into place, and what works here will vary from person to person. My daughter has severe ADHD, and her life is run on Post-it notes. I had no idea they came in so many colours, but the system works for her – all it does for me is decorate my house with neon confetti.

Keep important documents together. We have a series of paper file envelopes, labelled Car, House, Ann Health, etc, and all documents and letters get shoved into those. Every so often, I go through and sort them out, getting rid of unnecessary stuff and keeping whatever's relevant. Passports, insurance details and other seriously vital things are kept together in a large zip-lock bag in a drawer – in an emergency, I can grab that and go. I also have photos of those documents stored in the cloud, so that, if they get lost, I can find policy numbers, dates and details.

Managing your time

This sounds ridiculous to those who do not need it, but for those who do, ALWAYS enter appointments at a slightly earlier time. For example, if your dentist appointment is at 1pm, mark it on your calendar for 12.45pm – then you have a little leeway to check in, take off your coat or even deal with a small delay en route. Get into the habit of being early. Those of us who use public transport will be far more aware of the benefits of this than drivers, because a small delay at the start of a journey can translate to many hours at the end. Many years ago, I scored a train journey to my sister near Manchester for £7 each way, but it involved multiple changes, all quite tight on time. I left at 4pm and was due to arrive before 9pm. The first leg was delayed ten minutes, so I missed my connection, which left me thirty minutes behind. By the time I finally arrived, I was four hours late.

Allowing enough time for everything is a way to ensure you keep your stress levels low. Be realistic when look-ing at your timetable. It takes longer than five minutes to eat a slice of toast and drink a mug of tea, and ironing a shirt takes five minutes plus the time needed to put up the ironing board and heat the iron, while cleaning your teeth and having a shower takes twenty minutes if you are quick. All this means that if you climb out of bed just ten minutes before you need to leave the house, it generally means you'll be hungry and unkempt – or you'll be late. More than likely you'll be all of the above, and hot and flustered to boot. Then, if you drive, you'll be tempted to speed, and you may get a ticket. All of this is easily avoided by getting up in good time. If you struggle with that, just a thought – GO TO BED EARLIER!! I'd also suggest getting things ready the night before, as it minimises stress.

Sleep: the key to everything

You'll find it far easier to stay organised if you are well-rested

I discovered early on that I need nine hours' sleep to feel okay – I go to bed at 9pm, and wake naturally and easily at 6am. Margaret Thatcher famously claimed to only need four hours, but we all differ. To test if you are getting enough sleep at night, go into your bedroom in the day, draw the curtains and set an alarm for fifteen minutes' time, then close your eyes as if to sleep. If the alarm wakes you, it means you dozed off within 15 minutes and need more sleep at night. If you're still awake, you are probably okay. If you wake up four hours later having missed the alarm entirely, you are seriously sleep-deprived and absolutely need to deal with this. If you think you are getting sleep but are still exhausted, try using a sleep app to see how well you sleep – and Continuous Positive Airway Pressure (CPAP) machines for heavy snorers are truly a miracle.

Struggle to switch off? Try the following

Some people need more sleep but struggle to get to sleep in the first place, as they cannot turn off their brains. This happens to all of us occasionally, but if it persists it can become a real problem. Drugs don't help much beyond the very short term and are usually easy to become dependent on. Practising good 'sleep hygiene' is important. I do browse on my phone a bit, but I switch to a book on my Kindle app, and as soon as I start to doze off, I turn out the lights. An audiobook can work well, although you'll often find you end up listening to the same two chapters for months. There are lots of other methods to be found online, but one I find works extremely well is something called cognitive shuffling.

Think of a very neutral word – fairly long and with a selection of letters. I use 'chimpanzee'. Then I list animals beginning with 'c', and when I run out of ideas, I list animals beginning with 'h', and so on down the letters contained in 'chimpanzee'. I've never got past 'i for ibex'. If you're bad with animals, you can pick cities or types of fruit. It's irrelevant what the words and categories are, as you're just keeping your brain harmlessly occupied while you go to sleep.

However, in order for any of this to work, you need to be physically comfortable. You don't want to be hungry or thirsty, but, equally, eating or drinking immediately before sleep can cause you to bounce awake, needing a pee. Drinking alcohol is also a huge disruptor of sleep, so please, never think a drink before bed is helpful, as it will end up doing more harm than good. I suggest avoiding coffee or energy drinks after around 5pm as well. For many years I had a cigarette and a mug of coffee last thing at night, and although I got to sleep okay, I woke a lot in the night.

This leads me neatly on to other habits – when you are young, you absolutely should enjoy yourself. It's not obligatory to drink and party, as plenty of people hate that and always have, so, if that's not your bag, then do not let yourself be pushed into it. It's not cool, and there are other ways to enjoy life.

If you are a party animal, then by all means have fun, and enjoy it while youth lets you recover (I didn't go to bed for a week once – just went out clubbing, got home, washed and went back out to work), but please remember that the world is full of broken party people who discovered too late that the party was no longer fun. They woke up older but no wiser, with their health ruined and no money, no opportunities, and all too often a crippling addiction.

9

GENERAL LIFE ADVICE

Ironing: everything you need to know

I am a bad ironer – I hate it. It's boring and tedious. It has to be said, though, that to look groomed and put together, your clothes really need to be nicely ironed. I was at an event recently and noticed quite a few girls in lovely dresses that they had obviously simply removed from a packet and put on – and they looked rather tatty. A few moments with an iron would have transformed the outfit.

First thing: please do NOT iron on the floor, as a heated iron can cause expensive damage in seconds. If you do not have an ironing board, then use a table with several thick towels, as, again, the steam and heat from an iron cause a lot of damage quickly. Buy an ironing board if you iron more often than once a month, as it will make your life much easier.

How to handle different fabrics with your iron

Most modern irons are steam irons, and you should use distilled water to avoid them gunking up, but if you can't get that, then use the water from your kettle, as after it's boiled most of the minerals are left behind in the kettle. Better there than the iron, as a kettle is easy to descale.

Synthetic items must be ironed on a cool setting – please remember they are made from plastic, which melts at high temperatures. Pure cotton and linen will take heat, but polycotton will stick to the soleplate.

Use the steam, and as an extra insurance, use a cloth to protect the clothing (and the iron) – an old cotton tea towel kept especially for this is ideal.

Go steadily and don't rush. It's easier to press fabric that is slightly damp. I have been known to roll up some stuff when slightly damp and pop it in a bag, then store it in the freezer until I have time to iron.

To iron a shirt, you start with the collar, then the yoke, followed by the sleeves and cuffs, then the back, then the front – one side, then the other. This way, you avoid dragging a previously ironed bit on the floor any more than necessary. Hang until cool.

For trousers, start inside out to get the pockets smooth and flat, then iron the front underneath the pockets to ensure the shape of the pocket isn't ironed into the material. Turn right way round and finish the waistband and upper half. Be extremely careful not to press tram lines in – I gently press the crease both front and back, then use a cloth to press the seams, then I press the whole leg, as that seems to ensure I don't end up with either tram lines or a bunched seam on the leg.

If things such as knitwear need pressing, use a cloth, and steam but do not iron – pull to shape and press down for a moment, then lift the iron and move it over. This way, you avoid distorting the shape.

Navigating the dress-code minefield

Understanding formal dress codes

If you're invited to something and you're given a dress code, it's quite scary. If an invite states 'morning dress' or 'white tie', it will matter, and you may not be admitted if you dress down.

White tie

This you will have to rent, as if you already have a tailcoat in your wardrobe, you probably do not need this guide! This is the most formal dress code and not one to be messed with.

For gentlemen, you'll need a black tailcoat (this is not the same as a morning coat, as the cut is different), combined with black trousers with two lines of braid down the outside seam. You'll also need a white shirt with a detachable wing collar and double cuffs, closed with studs, along with a white bow tie (hand-tied), a white evening waistcoat, and plain, well-polished black lace-up shoes. This is not an occasion to try and stamp your personality on the outfit, as it's about quiet good taste, elegance and absolute tradition.

For women, white tie means a full-length evening gown, and bust out the jewellery (even a tiara, if you have one), but aim for elegance and traditional good taste – look at some old films for inspiration. A fur or an evening shawl is handy to keep yourself warm.

Morning dress

For gentlemen, this means a black or grey morning coat, plus grey or grey-and-black striped trousers, and a white shirt with a turndown collar, double cuffs and a tie. Over this goes a waistcoat in grey, light blue or buff. You can wear an understated handkerchief in your left-hand pocket.

For ladies, something smart is required – do keep your shoulders covered and do not go much shorter than just above the knee. A hat is not essential, but generally a welcome touch.

This is often the dress standard for weddings and people do stray from tradition here, but ONLY do so if you know the bride and groom are okay with this. Unless you are sure, stick firmly to tradition.

Black tie (also referred to as 'dinner jacket')

For gentlemen, this means a black wool dinner jacket (if not wool, at least make sure it's not shiny), which should be single-breasted (double-breasted with silk lapels is also acceptable), worn with black trousers with a single line of braid down the outside, a white evening shirt with a starched bib, double cuffs and a turndown collar, and a hand-tied bow tie. You may, if you wish, wear either a cummerbund OR a waistcoat. Think James Bond – avoid being anything other than elegant. A coloured waistcoat is acceptable, a coloured suit is not. Once again, stick to quiet elegance. Shoes should be plain well-polished black lace-ups. In Scotland, the kilt may be worn.

For ladies, dress up: it's not an occasion for a ball gown or a tiara, but an evening gown or a VERY elegant pair of trousers. Nothing too short or low-cut, but you are encouraged to look super glamorous.

*

Velvet jackets and bright cravats are out for all the above dress codes – you may see then on other men, but usually those men will be well known in that circle of people for their style. Again, if you need this guide, it's best to stick to it. Think how wonderful James Bond looks, and how tacky Austin Powers appears. Dress well and you can be confident you fit in – stand up straight, too! There is nothing worse than being at an event and feeling like an outsider. Being correctly dressed is camouflage, as it allows you to blend in while you find your feet.

Lounge suits

This simply means a suit, with a shirt and tie – no waist-coat. It is business dress, so look smart and well-pressed.

For ladies, this means anything smart – again, business dress.

Smart casual

A jacket or blazer with trousers, for men – chinos or cords are fine. You do not have to wear a tie and can leave your collar undone. If it's cold, a jumper is fine. Shoes can be lace-ups or loafers, but not trainers. On some occasions jeans are acceptable, but do ask first, and if in doubt, avoid.

For ladies, don't overdress: a smart day dress, or trousers with smart shoes, will be perfect. Keep jewellery simple.

*

The idea of dress codes can seem outdated, and in many ways they are, but they can also be a great leveller – if you stick to the code, you won't stand out. So be critical. Your clothes should fit well; if you're renting an outfit, make sure it fits properly. Make sure your hair is clean and tidy, your hands clean and manicured, your shoes clean and polished. Pay attention to the detail and you'll look amazing, and feel confident.

A beginner's guide to gardening

You may find you are in charge of a garden for the first time ever – it's tempting to just leave it alone, but I'd advise a little care, as rats and mice hang out in unkempt gardens, and while we need insects to thrive, you don't want mosquitos breeding in water-filled bins.

Dealing with brambles and nettles

I'm sure you don't need me to remind you that most plants grow in summer and die back in winter, so if you inherit a muddy patch with brambles in December, it's a good idea to tackle some of it then. Brambles are fast growers, no matter how often you cut them back, so it's a good idea to dig them out. When you do this, you may also see yellow rope-like roots growing close to the surface. These are very likely stinging nettles, so get rid of as many as possible before the spring sends them into active growth. Wear thick gloves while you deal with both of these. Both brambles and nettles are food plants for butterflies, and make excellent intruder deterrents, so maybe think about leaving a strip of several feet on one boundary but clear the rest.

Preparing for spring: pruning and raking

You may also have several buddleia bushes – dig up any you don't want, but do leave one. Cut it right back, though, as, like brambles and nettles, they grow fast. The beautiful flowers form on that year's growth, so a good hard prune every winter ensures lots of flowers (and hopefully clouds of butterflies, too).

Rake the soil level and wait for spring, as it's very possible there are plants under the scrub from a previously loved garden that you can resurrect. While things are low, have a look at your fence and see if you can cut a few hedgehog-sized gaps at the very bottom – these spiky chaps need to be able to travel from garden to garden and, with modern fences, that can be a problem – one that has contributed to their decline.

Weeds and grass: tips for maintaining a healthy lawn

Weeds are simply plants that grow where you don't want them – very often vigorous ones, which outcompete the ones you do want. If you decide you just want grass, just rake in grass seed as it starts to warm up, but remember you need to cut it every week, so you'll probably need a lawnmower. There is a labour-intensive process to getting a smooth and even lawn, but I've found that if you're not too fussy, you can just rake the surface fairly level then chuck down grass seed. The birds will eat plenty of it, but if you sow the seed just before a rainy spell in late spring or early summer, enough will sprout that, as long as you run the lawnmower over it regularly, you'll end up with a grassy patch. Remember dandelions are an early food plant for bees as well as being very pretty, so don't fuss too much about weeds.

The importance of wildlife-friendly gardens

Personally, I think a deeply planted perennial garden is easiest. You'll need to prune and weed every now and again, but choose your plants well and that's not an onerous job. You don't have to be too fussy about clearing leaves away either, as it's beneficial to insect life – and, by default, any other wildlife – to leave twiggy heaps and piles of leaves in which they can overwinter. If you want to know what to plant, have a nose around your local area to find out what does well, and if you feel confident enough, you can ask a gardener for a bit of root or a cutting, as they are often glad to get rid of them. Make a mental note of roughly where you saw them – in full sun, in shade, under a tree, etc – and put it in roughly the same place in your own garden. Place taller plants at the back towards the wall, graduating to lower ones at the front.

Perennials vs annuals: finding the right plants for your garden

I mentioned perennial plants earlier – these are plants that are tolerant of winter and will grow back every year. Annual plants (also known as bedding plants) die off every year and must be replaced in the early summer, but they are a cheap and colourful way to fill space in the garden while your perennials grow in. DO NOT PLANT CAT NIP – I did once, and woke to more London cats in my garden than I thought possible. Some were very unfriendly.

Despite what you may think, the plantless fully decked garden is hard work. You may think this will mean you won't have to deal with leaves and debris, but they will work their way in from somewhere, and decking can be extremely slippery unless kept clean, and terribly hot in summer. It also does not last as long as you might think – estimates online range from five to thirty years. The thirty-year estimate was from a company who – you guessed it – sell decking. They point out it depends on the conditions, and also how well you maintain it. I also need to say here that I think plastic grass is an abomination – it's another thing sold as an easy option when it is any-thing but. It needs cleaning regularly, it's incredibly hot in summer, if you slip and fall the grazes are horrendous, and it's barren. I understand the immediate appeal of these decked gardens with a scrap of Astroturf, but they are not maintenance-free, and provide nothing of value to wildlife – except for rats, who are very keen on the shelter they provide. I like rats as well as the next woman, but I don't want them colonising my garden. They cause a lot of damage.

Hosting: throwing a party

Housewarming parties are traditionally thrown before you replace the carpets, because it can really mess up your home if you have a rip-roaring boozy get-together. If you have a small group of well-behaved friends, it's perfectly possible to host an evening with no damage, but if they are a crowd of mess-heads, I suggest you think very carefully. The late A. A. Gill told the story of a student party held at someone's parents' house, in which the guests decided to bring the entire garden inside, dragging mud and plants over the carpet. They utterly destroyed both the garden and the house.

I cannot imagine the horror of the poor owners – their beloved home ruined because a party got out of hand.

Numbers and food

If you intend to host, then first decide on numbers. For numbers under around twenty, it's worth feeding people. If you can seat everyone, then a formal or semi-formal dinner party is possible. If not, then a buffet-style arrangement is good.

Don't be too adventurous with food. Stick to something you make well, and don't go for anything fiddly. If you want to impress with this year's fashionable dish, make sure you have cooked it several times beforehand. One hostess I know who throws fantastic parties does a huge pot of rice, another of curry, chilli or bolognese, and a mushroom stroganoff, all in slow cookers. It gets put out at around 10–10.30pm, as people are well oiled by then but not totally trashed. Everyone helps themselves and it slows the drinking nicely. It's all cooked in advance, so she's not stressed. A pile of disposable bowls and napkins also means the clean-up is easy.

A traditional dinner-party set-up

If you are sitting around a table to eat, you can have the more traditional dinner party set-up of a starter, main and pudding – but, once again, try not to do anything too tricky, as easy dishes done well are always well received. The very retro 1970s menu of prawn cocktail, coq au vin and black forest gateau was popular not only because it was delicious if cooked well, but also because it was easy to prepare in advance, leaving the hostess free to entertain her guests. If you stick to food you can at least partially prepare in advance, that you can cook well, and that you know will be well received, you'll find it much easier to relax and enjoy the evening. If something goes disastrously wrong, own it, laugh, and move on. It will become a tale to tell at other parties.

A drinks party set-up

Drinks parties can be either a lunchtime or cocktail party, so give people an arrival time but also advise them when to leave (carriages at 2pm, say) – a well-tried formula is to invite a crowd for drinks at 12pm, then have a few of those stay for lunch after. It's usual to give a finish time for evening parties, but it's far less likely that people will stick to it, for obvious reasons. A famous invitation from the Tolkiens to their son's twenty-first birthday party ended with: 'Carriages at midnight – Ambulances at 2 a.m. – Wheelbarrows at 5 a.m. – Hearses at daybreak'.

If you simply want a crowd round for drinks, then prepare in advance – invite your guests and do ask them to RSVP, so you have an idea of numbers. You can hire glasses, as you're unlikely to have enough. Some places offer free hire if you buy the wine from them, but they do usually want a deposit per glass, so check out what is available near you. Plastic glasses or cups are an alternative, and are a wise idea if things are likely to get rowdy – broken glass is not what you want to be dealing with when you have a hangover.

Preparation is key: the dos and don'ts of party preparation

Order your booze in advance. Don't get spirits – stick to wine or beer. If you have carpets, I suggest white wine only. A bottle of wine or champagne gives six glasses per bottle, while a 330ml can or bottle of beer is a mugful. Work out what you think agreeable. Ask people to bring a bottle, but be aware plenty will bring nasty cheap stuff no one wants to drink, then tuck into your nice wine.

My mother used to keep a bottle of good malt whisky buried in a bin of rice in the pantry, and only a few guests were in the know.

Warn your neighbours. If practical, invite them to come, as no one is going to complain about a party they attended.

Fill a few flexi tubs with ice, salt and water to act as chillers. Then move everything breakable safely out of the way. If it's likely to be a big crowd, consider booking a carpet-cleaner for a few days later.

Lay out bowls of nibbles if you aren't feeding people – they'll serve as blotting paper to soak up a bit of booze. Crisps, nuts, etc are fine, but I'd avoid those bright yellow cheesy things, as the yellow colour is difficult to remove if it gets on carpet or flooring. Pick your playlist and put it on. Not too loudly at first, as hopefully people will want to chat – the volume can go up later. A good rule is to start with enough light so people can see each other, and music low so they can get acquainted, but as the evening goes on, you can turn the lights down and the music up.

If things start to get out of hand, try to evict gatecrashers and close the door firmly to stop people coming in uninvited, but please don't hesitate to call the police for back-up if you feel unsafe in any way. Honestly, parties do get completely out of hand, and if it's your home (or your parents' home) you are under no obligation to entertain people you don't know, don't like and who are behaving inappropriately. Far better to call for help than hope things will work out okay – they rarely do.

The best parties end at daybreak with a small group of friends talking quietly as they fall asleep on the sofas, the bulk of the guests having left hours ago. Drink a pint of water (or Dioralyte) before you go to bed.

The morning after

The next day, get a good breakfast into you – you need fat, and a pint of tea with sugar – then face the clean-up. Hopefully it's not too bad.

Owning a pet

I'm militant about some things, and one of them is pet ownership. Very few animals are suitable as pets, and all pets need more money and time spent caring for them than is expected. No matter what you keep, PETS ARE EXPENSIVE.

Small animals: hamsters, mice, guinea pigs and rabbits

Hamsters, mice and rats need large cages – huge cages. They also need a lot of enrichment and care. Putting them in the tiny cages sold at pet shops is cruel, and they are completely unsuitable pets for children. They bite, and being squeezed will kill them. You also need to be absolutely certain what sex they are, or your two sweet mice will turn into fifty mice very very quickly.

The same applies to guinea pigs and rabbits – they need a lot of space, regular, GENTLE handling and a varied diet. Rabbits need regular myxomatosis vaccinations, and both guinea pigs and rabbits can be hard to sex. It's the same deal as small rodents: it's a good idea to keep them in pairs for company (in fact, it's illegal in Switzerland to keep a lone guinea pig, as they are social animals), but it's also easy for the breeding to get out of hand, as they come to sexual maturity at around fourteen weeks. I'd advise having them spayed or neutered to make quite sure you're not going to struggle with too many.

Their housing needs to be secure – all animals can be persistent when trying to escape, and incredibly difficult to find and catch when they do. If they do escape, they can die slow and horrible deaths.

Cats and dogs

Both cats and dogs have been companions of humans for millennia, but still require adequate care, and that can be expensive. Whether you adopt or buy from a breeder, it's vital you get an animal who suits your lifestyle – do not get a Malinois or a Border Collie unless you have time and energy to train it, exercise it and keep its mind occupied. Many dogs are given up when they simply do not fit into the person's way of life. High-energy breeds, such as spaniels often prove unsuitable for people with busy or sedentary lifestyles.

Adoption vs breeding

If you buy from a breeder, do your research and check out the genetics. For example, a merle, or a curly-coated French bulldog, should not exist. Do not buy one, no matter how pretty they look. Make sure you see both parents. If it's a pedigree, then look carefully at the paperwork and check out the lineage. Look at things such as hip score in Labradors, and look at the home when you go to visit your potential future pet. Is it clean? Do the dogs look bright-eyed and healthy? If not, do not buy a dog because you feel sorry for it (a call to the RSPCA won't go amiss, though), as they will breed more. A licence is needed to breed more than three litters in a twelve-month period, so if you have reason to believe that this is happening, ask to see the licence. Your local council issues these licences, so if you suspect the breeder is breeding more litters than allowed, and they don't have a licence, report them. There is a lot of money in breeding, and sadly many people lack compassion and scruples, and thousands of animals suffer every year.

Genetics affect behaviour as much as they affect looks – Staffies, for example, are great with people, but not so great with other dogs – some more so than others. Greyhounds are like big cats, but are bred to chase small, fluffy things, which is why so many have to wear muzzles as a condition of rescue – no matter how loving and gentle your greyhound is, it has the potential to catch (and kill) a cat in seconds.

A poorly bred dog will have ongoing health issues, and very likely temperament problems too – genetics matter, despite the idea that it's all about the owners. I agree that a brutalised dog will have huge behavioural issues, but so can a badly bred one, sometimes because they are in pain or discomfort. Speak to a vet – they would far rather you spoke to them in advance about a breed than have to euthanise your dog in a year or so. And if you do have to euthanise your pet, please stay with it; let it hear your voice, and be on your lap.

There are similar issues with cats – no matter how adorable they look, some breeds have health issues. Scottish Folds, for example, have a body-wide collagen defect, and they are often in pain. They have a condition called osteochondrodysplasia, which causes fusing of joints, and can lead to a complete inability to jump or walk. Flat-faced cats, like flat-faced dogs, struggle to breathe. In fact, many popular breeds have serious health issues. Please don't shop on looks alone.

Kitten mills exist as well as puppy mills, so if you see adverts for kittens, please go and see them – and look for evidence that the cats actually live there and haven't just been brought in for the viewing.

Adopting animals from a shelter can be a good idea, as usually the shelters try to ensure a good fit between the animal and human. Many insist on only adopting within a certain radius and have quite high requirements. Very often these seem too high, but they are usually born from experience of having animals returned to them, or adopting out animals that subsequently escape a garden with low fences and are killed on the road. Be careful, though – one shelter in the UK was discovered to be importing puppies from puppy mills in Ireland, so not all animal rescue centres are acting in the best interests of dogs and cats. The same concept of knowing your breed applies when adopting – not all badly behaved dogs have been abused. Many have been in households that were totally unsuitable, have had little socialisation and have consequently been given up as the family cannot cope with them. Sometimes these problems are not fixable. I love my dog Hollie to the moon and back, but I adopted her as an adult, and she is not good with others. She remains an anxious, agoraphobic dog who will not leave the house without me, and who will not walk far from home.

Roaming and training

There is a huge argument online about whether cats should be indoor only or allowed to roam, much of it an argument between the USA and the UK. In the UK it is normal for cats to roam, but it does put them at risk of being killed on the roads, and I find it irritating when two of the furry killing machines from the houses behind me target the birds in my garden. However, it's argued that we lack predators in this country, and cats are only filling an ecological gap. Also, it's said that many cats need to roam to be happy. Houses in the UK are far smaller than many in the USA, and we do not have coyotes or other large apex predators either. To be fair, it could be argued the car fills this niche, but that is another argument entirely.

There was a time when dogs, as cats, used to just wander around the neighbourhood. Over time, that habit has gone, due to increased traffic and the way we view our animals, and that may well be what happens with cats too.

Dogs need training, and they need socialisation to be calm and happy. But they must be under your control at all times, which means an off-lead dog must come when you call – first time, every time. I've owned a dog that did not like other dogs and attacked an off-lead terrier that came bounding up to him, despite me yelling for the oblivious owner to call it away. Luckily, it only needed a few stitches, but it could easily have been worse.

Understanding your dog's needs

Make sure you have the time for your dog – it's infuriating when people get a sociable dog, leave it alone for eight hours a day, then get rid of it because it ripped up the house. It's not just physical exercise. I mentioned earlier that spaniels are high-energy; you can walk them until your feet ache, and yet they still race around like mad things. However, set them to do what they were bred for, by getting them to retrieve toys that you've hidden, and they will sleep like fluffy angels when they get home because their brains did some work. Most dog breeds are bred for a purpose – allow them to fulfil that purpose, and they will be happy.

Pet safety and identification

Ensure your animal is chipped – it's a legal requirement. Also make sure that, if you move house or change your phone number, that the chip is updated with your new details. If an animal has a collar and there is a risk it could get caught on the collar, then think about a breakaway collar – these are usually for cats, but occasionally a dog will need one. Think about putting an air tag in your dog's harness – that way, if it runs off, you stand a chance of finding it. We live in the New Forest, and every month dogs set off in hot pursuit of deer – sadly, many are not recovered.

I suggest using a harness for your dog rather than a collar, as it's more secure, and if it's brightly coloured, it's easier to spot your dog from a distance. They usually have reflective patches, which of course helps with visibility after dark. I have a stout lead for Hollie, which is around four feet in length, with an additional handle closer to her body, so if I need to hold her securely by my side, I can. I hate extendable leads, as I'm forever seeing dogs racing around while their owners frantically try to reel them in. A far better solution is to have two leads: a shorter one for walking near roads or in busy places, and a long-line one for more remote walks. It means your dog cannot run off after a deer if it sees one, but still has plenty of freedom to snuffle and explore.

Register your animal with a vet. I discussed pet insurance in an earlier chapter (see p. 26), but if you decide not to insure, then be aware veterinary care is expensive. Hollie had to be anaesthetised for an X-ray recently and it cost £800.

After all that, you need to provide good-quality food – and be aware that, just as charlatans push unhealthy and unsuitable diets and supplements on humans, they also do the same to our animals, so try not to fall for overpriced nonsense.

Reptiles and fish: trust the specialists

I have no experience of either, but I can tell you this: they need quite specialist care, and unless you are confident you can provide this, then don't bother. Make completely sure you know all about them before you start. I know reptiles in particular are very sensitive about their environment, and a good vivarium costs a lot of money. Some lizards and snakes grow to prodigious sizes, too, so please be aware of that! Like that cute, fluffy puppy that ends up the size of a horse, that sweet little Burmese python can grow up to eight feet in a year.

Commit to your pet

Whatever animal you decide to get, it's essential you spend time in advance doing the necessary research. There is no excuse for getting a pet and then neglecting it. All living beings deserve care and respect.

How to deal with romantic break-ups

The first time you suffer a break-up, you think you will die from heartache. First loves are so very intense. After twenty-five similar bust-ups, you are far more robust – but it still hurts. Thankfully, there are tricks to help.

Love is just chemistry and chemistry fades

Firstly, please remember that falling in love is brain chemicals – dopamine, noradrenaline, and phenylethylamine – and these account for the strong feelings you have around your crush. It's a physical reaction, and like many physical reactions, it wears off. Your brain is flooded with feel-good chemicals, then, after a while, they trickle away to nothing. Sometimes it can last months, sometimes only a week or so. Many of us know that awful realisation that a strong attraction has died – often quite suddenly – and the person you would have given your eye teeth to spend a week in bed with is actually now boring and annoying. It's normal and it happens. Sadly, of course, it generally happens for one half of a couple before the other.

Long-term relationships: it's not always fireworks

If you are lucky, you will have forged a stronger bond; a deeper, more lasting emotion will have replaced what was initially just lust, and you won't really notice when that initial spurt of attraction wears off. In the long term, you need less of a dynamite sex partner and more of a trusted best friend, although sex still matters.

When you speak to people who have been together for decades, they will often say that quite long periods of time passed when they couldn't stand their partner, but they stuck with it and it came right. Often sex helps, though – it's a glue that sticks you together while you rebuild the rest.

When it's over, it's over – and that's okay

Sadly, break-ups do happen – you fell in love, the love wore off, and one of you disappeared to pastures new. Mutual break-ups are the easiest to cope with. It's sad, and for the first week or so you feel really bloody, but after the worst is over and you look back, it's hard to see why you were so devastated. If you were left for another person, that's hurtful in the extreme – and for obvious reasons, it's harder to get over. You will get over it, though. I promise.

Save your dignity: no drunk texting

Tips here involve deleting their number – blocking it, if needs be. Anything you need to do to avoid drunk texting them at 2 am. If you're really prone to this, then give your phone to a friend for the night. If you do text, your dignity will be destroyed; you'll just look a fool and it won't gain you anything. Allow yourself a day to howl and snivel all you like, then have a bath and indulge yourself with lots of nice little treats. Avoid the booze, though – it won't help. In fact it'll make you feel terrible.

Keep busy, keep moving

Now you simply need to keep yourself occupied while it wears off – and it does wear off. Keep busy, do things you enjoy that were impossible when you were a couple, see your friends, and make a point of reminding yourself how much fun you can have. If they crop up in your head (which they will do), remind yourself how they chewed with their mouth open, let out a squeaky fart every time they peed, and insisted on using your toothbrush. This was never going to work: it's sad, but it's far better now than later down the line. I promise you will live.

Connect with friends – several groups, if possible. You need a person with whom to get horrifically pissed, delve into the character of the ex and find every flaw; someone who will allow you to design wonderfully complicated plans for revenge, but (and this is ESSENTIAL) will not permit you to go through with them. You also need someone with whom to let out the hurt and anger without creating havoc in the rest of your life – because while the idea of going full Carrie Underwood (look it up) sounds appealing, that kind of stuff has a nasty habit of catching up to you a few months down the line when you are feeling much better, have moved on and are quite happy. Being arrested for criminal damage won't make your life run any better. Then there's the interesting and sensible friend: someone to make sure you eat well and to accompany you on bike rides and to films. This friend can help you fill in a Hinge profile, then show you how to set the filter to remove unwanted anatomical photographs and weed out the horrors. By the way, when on blind dates, ALWAYS let a friend know your plans, turn on location sharing, and arrange an emergency phone call at around the one-hour mark, so if you need to leave they have a pre-planned emergency ready. Don't make it too serious, though, or you might get pressed into accepting a lift. Lastly, you need someone with whom to giggle through the whole thing: the break up, the awful dates, the fact he left with your corkscrew (this actually happened to me – it was a disaster, as I drank a bottle of gin instead of wine, with the expected results, and it was years before I could touch gin again).

The take away from all this is that you can manage a break-up, and you can retain your dignity while you're doing it, and, with time, this will all become another amusing story to tell!

The hard break-ups: when your lives are entwined

When break-ups happen later on, it's more difficult, as you often have a life together, maybe even children, and untangling it all is painful. It's hard even if the split is mutual. People change over time; their perspective and priorities change, and sometimes couples realise there is simply no point – that they're low-level miserable all the time. Once again, the difficulty happens when one partner realises this when the other is perfectly happy. The thing here is to realise that if your partner is miserable, and you thought things were okay, the relationship wasn't as good as you thought; you weren't communicating the way you should have been, and possibly you didn't trust each other like you should.

First thing is to find out if this is fixable – sometimes, with a LOT of talking, and a large dose of compromise and forgiveness, you can dig yourselves out of the rut you have worn and reinvigorate things. If that's the route you take, may I advise professional counselling? It helps guide your discussion and stops it degenerating into petty bickering. A good counsellor may also be clear-headed enough to realise the relationship cannot or should not be saved, and can help both of you navigate that with as little rancour as possible.

If it's not recoverable, and that's your choice, then it's shattering news. Firstly, if you have children, a word of advice: you are both parents and will remain so, so you will always be connected by your children. Never, ever utter a word of criticism about your partner to your children. If your partner is a terrible person, if they have behaved in the worst possible way, then your children will work it out on their own, but if you keep putting the boot in, they will resent you. Keep that for a few trusted friends. Divorce is now no-fault, and things are split pretty much 50/50. I advise you consult a good family law specialist if you are married or in a civil partnership, in order to be certain the financial arrangement is fair and final. There are different options for this in Scotland and Northern Ireland, but it's a good rule in life to always consult a solicitor when money or property is involved.

If you are not married, you can still apply to the courts to uphold visitation and financial support for the children –

as I said previously, the law puts the wellbeing of children above all else – and, quite frankly, so should both of you.

Emotionally, it takes a long time to get over the breakdown of a long relationship, and that's especially hard to do if things get acrimonious – but you will get over it. The same things help as before: keep busy, keep your dignity, and try to build your new life in the way that suits you. Small consolations can be played up – perhaps, finally, you can have pure white bedlinen, or sleep with the window open in January? I have found myself single twice, both times after breaking up with men who were terrible with money, and one of the biggest reliefs was the knowledge I could pay bills and still have enough in the bank for food, and that my earnings were MY earnings, and not being spaffed in the pub by others. Think of these things with relief. If you are childless and hate coming home to an empty house, consider letting a room (do check the legality here, though, to be safe) or getting a cat. One thing I can promise you is that you will get over the break-up, as long as you don't fall into the trap of nurturing your upset, which is all too easy to do. Nurture yourself, not your resentment, and learn to love your own company, to really grow into yourself. If you are thinking about another relationship, it's easier to have a satisfying one if you are true to yourself. You are less likely to become subsumed in the personality of another. The other side of this, of course, is that lively, confident people are often more attractive. You may find you don't want another relationship – many people don't, and the single life has much to recommend it.

The single life: underrated, and healthier than you think

The trope of single cat ladies has been overplayed, but don't forget that, statistically, single women live longer than married women, but married men live longer than single men. Often that is because women build strong bonds with people, not just family, so when they find themselves alone, they have a support network. Men, on the other hand, often lack those connections, so when they find themselves alone, they are terribly lonely.

Studies have been done that show those with religious affiliations enjoy measurable health benefits. That hasn't got much to do with the religion itself, as it is noticed across faiths, and persists when factors such as alcohol consumption and sexual moderation are take into account. It seems that the key factor in this is social connection; those who attend a place of worship regularly make social connections. Those connections can be made without the need for attending church, however – find either a cause or a hobby you can truly commit to and join in. These connections support you in times of crisis, but you can and should forge them at any time, even though it sometimes appears impossible. I'm a huge believer in being a volunteer, and most places have all sorts of options available. Local am-dram groups are often full of lots of would-be stars but short on behind-the-scenes helpers. Dog shelters, meanwhile, always need people to shovel poo. Don't look for glamour, as very often it's the down-to-earth they need. Doesn't matter what it is, as if you feel wanted and needed, and can meet like-minded people, you are onto a winner!

Friendship break-ups: just as painful but sometimes necessary

In someways I should have covered friendship break-ups alongside relationship break-ups because the process is similar. The reason I put it here is that we tend to think of friendships as more enduring. We all have people we've lost touch with. That's normal; as life moves onwards, we lose contact with people. But sometimes you have a friend, or a friendship group, and you realise they are not what you want anymore – either they are actively harmful, or you simply have nothing in common with them any longer and feel like you are wasting time and energy with people who add nothing to your life. Often it's easier to just drift away; you don't accept invitations, or don't answer the phone as much. You might unfriend them on social media, or untag yourself in photos. Sometimes you realise you are doing all the work, and all you need to do is stop putting in the effort. Within a few months, you are distant enough to relax. Ghosting, though – as that's what this is – can be deeply unpleasant and you do sometimes have to make a point of telling someone you will not be in their life anymore.

Confronting the end of a friendship

It can be difficult when you need to confront someone, or when you are confronted. Being told someone no longer wants to be your friend is devastating: you feel you must be worthless and unlovable. Neither is true. It's simply that, as I've said before, people change. It's not bad that people change, it's natural, but that means they grow apart. If a friend has told you they no longer want contact with you, it's hurtful, but (odd as this may seem) not personal. It's about both of you changing, and sometimes that means behaviour you both took as normal has become difficult for one of you.

For some years, I had a friend who was nothing but kind, but after a while that kindness started to feel oppressive and patronising. I found constantly being grateful became difficult, because if I didn't acknowledge the kindness effusively, I was reminded until I did. I chose to break away, and felt incredibly guilty about it. Of course they didn't understand what they had done wrong, and explaining it was impossible. I chose not to explain, as there was no way I could do that without causing a deep hurt. Once the obligation of our friendship was broken, I realised it wasn't about me; they were simply someone who needed desperately to be loved and needed due to their own insecurities, and I could not fulfil that. Nor did I want to. You don't always need to be brutal – and if you do decide to tell them why, be kind with it.

Standing up for yourself and setting boundaries

Following on from this, it's worth talking about standing up for yourself and setting boundaries. Often, you hear that boundaries are for other people to be aware of – as in, 'I set a boundary, how dare they break it?' – but boundaries are actually for you to act upon. For example, you might tell your friend you cannot have her telephoning you at all hours of day and night. You might explain you are free to chat after work and up until bedtime a few times a week, and, if that's not enough, and she keeps hounding you with calls, you will block her number. So, you set the boundary, you make it clear, and you explain what will happen if she breaks the boundary. The next day she calls you at work, so you ask her not to ring again, tell her you will ring later, and remind her you will block her if she continues. She rings again an hour later, so you block her number and move on with your day. There is no further explanation needed, as you made it plain. It's up to you if you choose to ring back after work or not, but now you know you will no longer be disturbed.

There is no need to get angry, and no need for a row: you simply explain politely what the issue is, and continue – it's up to them if they persist in the behaviour, but they know the consequence. Obviously, this can make people very angry indeed, but that's not your problem – stick to being polite and firm, and don't budge. If they persist in trying to argue, then refuse to engage.

Saying 'no' without guilt

No, as people often tell you, is a complete sentence – you are not obliged to explain. You might want to, of course, and there are plenty of circumstances where that is the polite thing to do, but it's not obligatory.

'Can you work on Tuesday?'

'No, it's my day off.'

'It's really important, can't you change it?'

Now, you can offer an explanation here as to why you are sticking to your day off, but that leaves you open to wrangling about how important those plans are. You might figure you can move them; you want to oblige, in which case you can change your mind. But you have already refused, so you do not need to offer an explanation and open yourself up to that – you can just politely say: 'No, I'm sorry. It's my day off. I cannot change it.'

The trick is be polite but firm. Again, this can make people very angry – they may threaten you (you might want to check if these threats have validity – can they fire you? Will they fire you? Do you care?), but the trick is to remain calm and polite, which can be difficult to do but is worth it going forwards. Usually, once people understand that you cannot to bullied or manipulated, they become far more reasonable in future.

Enough is enough

All of the above – work, friendships, relationships – may require you to clearly and firmly say that enough is enough. Work is usually the easiest, as there should be a contract that specifies the amount of notice you need to give, and if you are determined to leave, you merely need to send an email saying something along the lines of:

Dear Ms Trunchbull,
Please accept this as my two-month notice, as required by my contract of employment. It has a been a pleasure working with you and I wish you and the school the very best going forward.
Thank you, Miss Honey

There is no requirement to give a reason, although if asked, you might wish to give one. You are expected to work as usual until your last day, but some companies will decide they will pay you to leave early, while others will want you to train your replacement. If that is the case, you are not obliged to work a day over your notice period in order to do that. If they politely request that, and you are not due to start elsewhere the next day, you can decide you wish to be obliging, but I suggest you get the agreement in writing. It is illegal to give a bad reference on subjective grounds. If they hate you, they can refuse to give you a reference, but they cannot write to any future employer and say you are lazy, incompetent and overly nice to small, strange girls.

Now, friendships and break-ups are a less formal version of that, and obviously emailing your partner with a date of termination is odd, but sitting down somewhere neutral and kindly but firmly explaining that the relationship is no longer working well for you, and that you are moving on, is the equivalent. Again, there's no need to go into detail (although some explanation is reasonable); just explain you've had a wonderful year, say, and that they will always remain special to you, but your feelings have changed, and you feel it would be better to make the break now rather than later. Obviously this can go incredibly badly, with tears and tantrums (hence why a neutral space is advisable), but you can let them feel their upset (and anger, which may involve name-calling) and empathise with that hurt. Just remain firm. It is not your wish to hurt them, but unfortunately it's inevitable, and you cannot continue now your feelings have changed. No, you can't give it another chance, as you have thought long and hard about it.

If they become threatening and aggressive, make sure you are safe, and if that continues past an initial tantrum, then call the police – if you feel they are likely to get difficult, and they have keys to your home (assuming you don't live together, that is), then it might be prudent to change the locks before the conversation.

Then ensure you reclaim that which is yours, and give them that which is theirs.

Ending friendships can be the same, but less intense – decline invitations and explain why, i.e. 'Thank you for the wedding invitation. It's much appreciated, but I will be unable to attend. I noticed on your hen do that our lives have started to separate and, in future, it may be best if we did not associate. You are a wonderful woman, and I hope your marriage is a resounding success.'

All this sounds very stiff and formal, but it's about giving you the general idea – be polite, kind and not over detailed. Care enough to let people down gently but firmly.

Lastly . . .

All of the above is based on the assumption that you are being reasonable, and it's incredibly important in life to have insight into your own behaviour. Very often the loudest bullies act with complete conviction that they are correct. Do be sure you are being sensible.

Caring for the elderly

The elderly often experience a little thing called forget-fulness: sometimes you will notice an older relative starts to become forgetful or starts acting very strangely. It's easy to panic and assume this means dementia, so let's take a breath here. Forgetfulness and woolly thinking are common as people age. People in their eighties are not always as quick-thinking as they were in their youth, and this isn't a problem unless it puts them in danger. In any case, there are aids and ideas than can help an older relative maintain independence while keeping them safe. I always tell people to get into the habit of using these aids long before they need them, as once your memory starts becoming unreliable, it's impossible to remember a new thing, but habitually setting a kitchen timer, if it's embedded, is suddenly essential. Hand rails and safe flooring are also beneficial early in proceedings, by the way.

Common issues among the elderly

Often the elderly exhibit symptoms that have easily treat-able causes – urine infections, for example, are notorious for turning previous sensible and rational people into complete lunatics in hours. Thankfully they are easily treated with a course of antibiotics and a little attention to self-care going forwards. Low iron, poor diet, medications being out of whack or the onset of a new problem can all cause our elders to become confused and disorientated, and all of these things are easily reversible.

Generally speaking, people should not start exhibiting symptoms of age-related decline until at least fifty, but more usually this doesn't become noticeable until a person reaches their seventies. Always see a doctor, because, as noted above, it's often something that can be helped. If not, then the earlier people take steps, the easier life will be going forwards. Of course, getting help for a furiously angry gentleman of seventy-five who believes someone is stealing his socks can be challenging if you don't know their doctor and are not related. I say this because one gentleman I knew started charging out of his house without warning and screaming abuse at people for no obvious reason. He had always been irritable, and the poor neighbours found it very difficult to access help. The first phone call was to the local doctors' surgery – and that can be a bit frustrating and a dead end, because doctors have a duty of care that involves keeping anyone's information confidential. So all you can do is ring and inform them, but don't expect to get much information back from them. If that doesn't seem to help, then you can contact your local police on 101 – ask them to do a welfare check, and explain you have notified a GP but are not a relative. They have more powers to intervene if they think it's necessary, and will know who to liaise with to get help. Even if you ARE a relative, you may not get much more information back unless the person is deemed to have lost capacity. Capacity is, broadly speaking, the ability to make choices for oneself, and it's difficult to assess, as well as changing all the time. It's frustrating for everyone when people who are acting highly irrationally are just left. It's difficult, because a foundation of our society is that you cannot just be deprived of your liberty without a very good reason. People are allowed to believe strange things and have odd habits – we only try to intervene if those habits are harmful to others, or to the person who has them. If your great aunt is happy and healthy while believing Winston Churchill is talking to her through her clock, you may well find it concerning, and wish to keep an eye on her, but that belief is harming no one. Millions believe in astrology, after all, and we do not medicate them.

Supporting the elderly: respect, understanding and planning ahead

If your elderly relative obviously needs help, but is resistant to it, please remember it is difficult for a person who has been capable and robust to accept they may be becoming frail and in need of help. Don't talk to them like a child – they are fully grown adults, with experience and an entire life behind them. They may struggle with new things, but that does not mean they are simple. Talk to them and try to understand why they won't accept help. Sometimes there's a simple reason. Can you compromise? Something else to consider is whether you could set up a lasting power of attorney (LPA) with them – I have one and it took around six months to be arranged, so it's as well to think ahead. It's a form registered with the Office of the Public Guardian, and means that if some-one becomes incapacitated and unable to manage their affairs, you can step in. It's well regulated and does NOT mean you can sell their house from under them, but it does mean you can look after their affairs if necessary – either permanently, in case of something like dementia, or temporarily, in case of a serious illness. You can get details on the GOV.UK site, but it is something that can be registered and then sit in a drawer for years until needed. I have one set up so that, if I become ill, my daughter can act on my behalf to ensure the rent gets paid, the taxman doesn't freeze my accounts, and my world oper-ates smoothly.

Death and dying

People die – everyone will die at some point, including you. It's normal and not to be feared. A few generations ago, death happened at home, and most people had contact with death from childhood. It was discussed and dealt with in the same way that marriage and childbirth were dealt with, as an inevitable part of life that simply needed to be handled. In more recent times, it has become almost taboo to discuss death, and we try to hide the dying away in hospitals. Many people have never seen a dead body. I think, in the USA, they often display a well-embalmed corpse at the funeral, but that's not common practice here. All of this means that people are woefully unprepared for what happens when a relative or parent dies.

Caring for a dying loved one

Due to a lack of hospice beds, many more people are likely to have their final weeks at home, and that's wonderful, but only if you can get the right care for them as they start to fail.

However, you may simply have an old and frail grandmother who is reasonably mentally alert and simply unaware of the fact she may need a degree of care. You can see she needs help, but are unsure how to go about getting it.

There is a division between medical care – administering medicines, prescribing new tablets, etc – and physical care – washing, dressing, feeding, etc. While there is a link between the two, they are dealt with by different people. The place to start looking for help is with your loved one's GP. If possible and practical, you'll want to ask if the person you're caring for will allow medical people to speak to you regarding their care (this is more straightforward with your granny, but probably not appropriate for a neighbour). This is known as 'consent to share', and without it, medical personnel will be unable to tell you anything, as they take confidentiality very seriously. There will be a form for the patient to fill in and sign, and they can withdraw consent at any time. If you have not got consent to share, that doesn't mean you cannot help – it's just the information will be one way.

In my area, we have people known as care navigators for the over-sixty-fives. At present they are not everywhere, and it is currently a trial role, but it's worth asking if your GP has one, and if not, who will be able to fulfil that function. A care navigator offers what they refer to as a person-centred approach – in other words, they need to assess the patient's needs and listen to their wants, as the two things are not necessarily the same. If they think the patient is at risk of harm, they can raise a safeguarding concern. If you are able, and the patient is okay with it, you may wish to sit in on any appointments, and hopefully the care navigator will be able to help with arranging necessary services.

In Hampshire there is a website called Connect To Support Hampshire, and it's highly possible your local council has set up something similar, so please ask. If not, have a look at my local one to work out what kind of help you may need, as it's worth understanding a bit about how it works even if the system is somewhat different where you are. The basic framework will be relatively similar, so it will give you an idea of what to ask for.

Talking about death

Once you have got care in place for someone, it's always a good idea to start talking – some people readily accept they are dying, and will want to plan a funeral and even talk about distributing their possessions. Other people absolutely refuse to make any reference to death, and that can be very difficult. You can have other conversations, though. Now is the time to go through the old photos and label them, so you know who all these people are. Record family stories, too. It is a source of endless regret that I did not make notes of things my grandmother told me about our family history, as I assumed I would remember it all, and of course, with time, I have forgotten. Record their voice, talk about things – even the difficult stuff – as this will be your last chance. Don't leave anything unsaid if you know you will regret it.

If they are bedbound, you can surreptitiously start clearing things. Obviously you may not dispose of their possessions, but the cupboard full of carrier bags and old margarine containers can probably be cleared. You can do things like tidying up and locating paperwork – all jobs which will have to be done at some point, and which will be made easier if you can put things in order in advance.

As death approaches

Sometimes people die quickly, other times you watch a slow decline. Once people have got to a certain point, they are usually either offered a hospice bed or given hospice care at home. This allows them to receive the care they need to end their life in comfort, and what this looks like obviously depends on their personal circumstances.

Hopefully you have had a chance to discuss with them what their wishes are for their funeral, although you do not need to be bound to that – funerals are expensive, and the one they choose may not be affordable. No one can be forced to pay for the funeral of another, unless they have signed the funeral contract.

What happens when someone dies at home

If someone dies at home and that death is expected, you need to phone their GP and their nearest relative (if that isn't you). The GP can come and certify they are dead. After this, you may need to contact a funeral director to remove the body and look after it until the funeral. It's wise to phone around and ask about prices if you haven't had a chance to do this before. Funeral directors are, by law, required to provide a standardised list of prices, so you can compare these to get an idea. It's also possible there is a prepaid funeral plan in place – if you're not sure, have a good look through any papers to see if you can find anything. While you don't need to panic and get the funeral director to come at once, you need to bear in mind that a modern heated house is not the best place to store a body (at the very least, turn off the radiators in the room). Funeral directors have the appropriate facilities and will treat the body with care and respect.

Required documents for registering a death

You must, by law, register the death within five days. You can neither bury nor cremate until this is done. Look up the location of the nearest registrar online, then phone and make an appointment.

You will need:

— the death certificate given to you by the GP

— their date and place of birth

— their address

— their occupation and whether they had retired

— whether they received any benefits (including a state pension)

Documents to support this will help:

— birth certificate

— NHS card or NHS number (found on letters from hospitals or doctors)

— passport

— marriage certificate

— driving licence

It is also useful to know the name, date of birth and date of death (if applicable) of their spouse or civil partner.

The registrar will give you:

— a green form for burial or cremation

— a death certificate

— a code for the Tell Us Once service (see below), along with some leaflets

You pay for the death certificate, and it is a good idea to pay for several extra copies, as some banks and other organisations will not accept photocopies, and it's more expensive and somewhat time-consuming to apply for extra copies later. Having said that, you can get too many, so try to think about or ask in advance how many you will need.

Informing organisations

The Tell Us Once service is incredibly useful, as it ensures all government departments get notified of the person's death in one go, but you'll still need to inform other organisations.

Pension providers, insurance companies, banks and building societies, utility companies, landlords, mortgage providers, dentist, local council . . . It's a long list, but in the main these organisations have a department dedicated to this, and they are helpful and sensitive.

Unexpected deaths

If someone dies unexpectedly, you need to phone 999 and explain what has happened. The death will need to be reported to the coroner, who will investigate the cause of death, and they may decide they require a post mortem to establish this. The police may call round and ask questions in order to help the coroner – all this is completely routine and nothing to worry about. You have no say in this, but if you need a quick funeral for religious reasons, you must let them know.

Funeral arrangements

You can organise a funeral yourself – I'm not going into this here, but it is possible, and can save a considerable amount of money. However, it needs careful organisation and it's important you comply with the law.

You can pay for the funeral yourself (although you are not obliged to), or it can be paid for from an insurance policy or the estate (this means the money and assets the person left behind). If you are on a low income, you may be entitled to a funeral expenses payment from the government of up to £1,000, but in my experience you may not get as much as you hoped for, as the Department for Work and Pensions take into account any money the person has.

If expense is a consideration, please make sure you let the funeral director know in advance, as they are experienced in this and will do their best to help. The cheapest option is usually something called direct cremation. The deceased is taken to the crematorium and cremated without attendants or ceremony at an unspecified time. You are notified after the event to collect the ashes. This is worth thinking about, as you can have a gathering to scatter the ashes or celebrate their life without having to pay professionals for their services. Be aware you cannot scatter ashes just anywhere, though, so please check in advance.

Dealing with the estate

This must be done whether the person left a will or not. If they did leave a will, they will have named an executor, and this is the person who is allowed to apply for probate.

Details of how to do all of this are to be found (once again) on the GOV.UK site – there are a lot of handy downloads and it's well worth spending a while looking through them.

If the deceased was renting their home, you may have an incredibly short amount of time to clear the property of their stuff, and house-clearance companies are expensive. You cannot be made to pay for the clearing of a place, however, unless you are named on the tenancy or are a guarantor. But the landlord can ask to use some or all of the deposit to pay for:

— last month's rent, if this was not paid

— the cost of clearing the property

If you and the landlord cannot agree, the deposit scheme will decide, and if the landlord incurs expenses over and above the deposit, they may expect to be paid from the tenant's estate. If they are not paid, they may ask the courts to investigate if the estate had money, and if so, they will ask to be paid from this. If you have disbursed money from the estate before all expenses are met, you may be liable yourself.

For details of how to deal with the death of a tenant, Shelter have useful information online.

Dealing with grief

Grief is a peculiar and difficult thing. The busywork surrounding death seems onerous and complicated, but it's very helpful. It gives you something practical to focus on while your brain deals with difficult emotions. If you are offered grief counselling, take it, as it helps. You will get over it, but you will never forget the person; you will find there will be moments you are overwhelmed by missing them, but, as time passes, those moments will become fewer, and instead you will remember them with pleasure. If you know someone who has a loved one who has died, let them talk. Don't avoid the subject, just let them reminisce – it helps a lot. In my experience, it's more difficult if your relationship with the deceased was poor, as there are a lot of emotions to process, and one thing that can really haunt you is that it is now finished – they (or you) can never apologise, or express your regret, or love.

Boundaries and beliefs

Another thing I will touch on here is that you are not obliged to have any contact with a dying person. Some of you may have decided to go no-contact with parents or siblings, and if you decide to keep that in place during and after death, do not feel guilty – deathbed reunions are not, in fact, very common in real life. People who are angry and bitter in life are angry and bitter when dying. It's okay to just ignore it. If you decided they were too toxic to let into your life while they were alive, there is no reason you should allow them into your life while they're dying – unless you feel you need to turn up and tell them they were abusive and cruel, that you do not forgive them. It may be that this would be closure for you.

Also, PLEASE do not proselytise – and if someone else tries to preach to you using a death as an excuse, you are allowed to tell them in no uncertain terms to boil their head.

What to do if you have a car accident

You MUST STOP! No matter how minor the crash, you must stop, switch off your engine and put on your hazard lights. Check no one is hurt – even slightly. Check all vehicles for damage. Exchange insurance details with the other driver(s), including names and addresses, and as much of their insurance information as they can manage.

If safe, take photographs of the vehicles and the surroundings.

If no one was injured and both vehicles are drivable, then, after this, if everyone is satisfied, you can continue your journey.

If anyone is seriously injured, if someone is in danger or if you believe an offence has been committed – for example, if you believe another driver may have been drinking, or if the accident has caused an obstruction, then call the emergency services at once to report this.

If the other driver does not stop, or refuses to give you their details, but everyone is uninjured, the accident is not causing an obstruction and no one is in danger, then stay where you are and phone 101 to report it. You can also report it online or at a police station, but you must do this within twenty-four hours of the collision.

Assuming you have exchanged details and have continued on your way, then you need to report to your insurance company as soon as possible. They will advise you of any further steps you need to take.

10

HOW TO SEEK HELP

Help is out there – it can be difficult to find, and frustrating to access at times, depending of course on what you are after, but is out there!

Health-related problems

When people need help with their mental health, they are often concerned that other people will find out – they feel shame that they are in this position. Please ignore this. Seek help as soon as you think you have a problem, as the faster you get help, the easier things are to deal with. It's a good first step to talk to your GP, but results can be variable: some GPs are brilliant, others terrible. They may pass you on to a talking therapy, or issue medication – or both. Having mental health difficulties is not something to be ashamed of. If you wouldn't be embarrassed about having a stomach upset, you shouldn't be embarrassed about depression. Yes, I know there is a stigma, but that stigma will not go away if we continue to uphold it.

Charities and self-help groups: you are not alone

There are a lot of useful charities and self-help groups, too – these can be invaluable to help you navigate a system that is frequently confusing and often fairly useless. Because the help is so incredibly variable depending where you are, I'm not going to make recommendations as such, but however isolated and alone you feel, I absolutely promise you, you aren't – there are others. No matter what you think, or how you feel – people care.

You can ring the Samaritans on 116 123 or contact them online – they are a kind, non-judgemental service. Talk to them. No matter how bleak the future seems, suicide is a permanent solution to a temporary problem.

Consent and confidentiality

Before we go any further, we need to cover something known as consent to share. I mentioned it briefly in the previous chapter (see p. 200), but it essentially means medical professionals cannot talk about us to anyone except other practitioners without our express consent, which we can withdraw at any time. If you confess you are severely mentally unwell, your doctor cannot inform your work, your parents or your college without you specifically consenting to this. The only exception is if your mental state puts other people at risk of harm. But if that is the case, they are more likely to admit you to hospital than to broadcast your problem.

This doesn't apply to children, but consent still has to be sought from the legal guardian. So if you are seeking help for anyone other than yourself, and there is not consent in place, it can seem as if no one is listening. They are, and they may even have a plan of action, but they cannot tell you about it. If the person you are concerned about is a family member, it can be distressing to discover you are being kept in the dark, but, sadly, family members are often responsible for horrendous abuse, so there's a reason the system is in place.

When friends or strangers need help, it can be easier – or impossible. If someone is sufficiently unwell that you are concerned they are a danger to themselves or others, you should contact the police on 101. Explain your concerns to them, and they can either conduct a welfare check (as explained on p. 194) or, in a dangerous situation, can detain someone under the Mental Health Act and take them to be evaluated by a doctor.

Advocating for yourself or for a loved one

If you, or someone you know, are suffering from a physical problem that does not seem to be getting dealt with in a satisfactory manner, it's important to advocate for yourself or them. Something I find incredibly helpful is to write down the problem – I do this first at length, and then, over a few drafts, I condense that information into key bullet points, ending with what I want as an outcome. This works because it enables doctors and health professionals to get the relevant information with a single glance, and it also ensures they understand what you want. And if they ignore some or all of what you are telling them, then it is easier to present the information to someone else and clearly state why you are dissatisfied with the outcome.

I recently had to do this for someone who was terminally ill. I'll outline it here to show how it worked. If it's for you, just follow the same formula.

The gentleman with a terminal illness was in pain but not willing to be admitted to hospital. He was struggling with care of his house, and his personal care. He was becoming confused with his medication and could no longer walk far enough to leave his home. The first thing we did was get our names put on his records, with that 'consent to share' note!

X is in pain, and can no longer manage his medications so they are efficacious; this is our most important point.

X cannot access help if he needs it, as he is unable to leave his home, and becomes confused if he tries to use the telephone.

X cannot care for his hygiene needs.

We need to get X's pain under control, and we need a doctor or nurse to visit at intervals to assess his health, to adjust or alter his medication if required and to address any further health needs.

We need in-home care to address his hygiene and his safety at home.

Getting proper care and following up

We started by speaking to the GP and the pharmacy, to organise home visits and get his medication pre-sorted in a dosette box, so he could take his tablets properly.

The GP passed his details to the community nurses, and they called once every two weeks to assess his wellbeing, and then, as he deteriorated, they came more frequently.

He was assessed for a care package – although people are expected to pay for in-home care if they have funds, the health authority will means-test and provide free help to those deemed in need but without funds. In this case, the care package was provided without charge.

We needed to be proactive in pushing for this, and it involved numerous phone calls to different branches of the NHS to find out who had responsibility. Stick to your bullet points – it stops people trying to evade your request. Sadly, the budgets in health and social care have been so severely cut that only the very desperate get help. Be polite, be firm and keep pushing – it's frustrating and infuriating that our health service is in this state, but the individuals within that service are generally trying their best. If you can work with them, and try to make their lives easier, you should get better results. If you become angry or abusive, they are well within their rights to refuse to deal with you. The same goes for carers – if your grand-father starts being abusive, then those caring for him are entitled to stop visiting him. One of my sons did care work and had several men who could only have male carers, as the abuse they meted out to the women was awful. Every-one deserves to have a safe work environment.

If someone is in hospital, then the ward clerk is a good place to start for any queries, as they can direct you to the relevant department and can help by explaining how the hospital system works – this is especially useful if the patient will need care after being discharged from hospital, and you have to make sure this is all in place. Again, please, please remember that they cannot share anything much with you unless the patient consents. Start by making certain that the details they hold are accurate, that the address on record is up to date, and that things like next of kin are listed correctly.

Ask them who the patient's consultant is, so that you know who will be responsible for the clinical decisions, and so you can be sure they are aware of all relevant information pertinent to their decisions. Ask when would be the best time to speak to that consultant, and check if the consultant is the best person for the queries you have. For example, if it's a query about food or day-to-day stuff, the nurse in charge will be a more appropriate person to approach. If you need to know about how the patient will cope after discharge, you may need to speak to the occupational health team.

Sometimes staff aren't aware of little things, and that can have unexpected results. I was in hospital some years ago and an elderly Asian lady was in the bed next to me. They struggled with her, as they couldn't get her to respond to questions, so assumed her English was poor. They got a translator in, who had very little luck, and everyone was upset and worried. They thought she might have dementia, and were talking about her going to a care home. A day later, her granddaughter arrived, and discovered that she simply didn't have her hearing aids in. Poor woman was as deaf as a post, and, yes, her English wasn't great, but as soon as she could hear people, she perked up, communication was restored and she was discovered to have a fine line in bad jokes.

The role of a GP

In the UK, our GP is the usual entry point into the health-care system. Unless you have an accident or emergency and go through A&E, you will need to speak to your GP. They can prescribe medicine, refer you for tests and direct you to appropriate consultants for more specialised help.

The Guardian Bookshop

J JEAN NALE
30 HARTWOOD ROAD
WEST CALDER

EH55 8DG
UNITED KINGDOM

THE GUARDIAN BOOKSHOP
PO BOX 48
WESTHAM, EAST SUSSEX
BN23 6WB

Thank you for ordering via
The Guardian Bookshop
We do hope you enjoy your product
If there are any issues please
contact us on
0203 176 3837 or
help@guardianbookshop.com

51169703

Order ID: [IOq3EpV2r9]   Carton: [HA007445689]   Order date: [23/09/2025]

UPC	TITLE	QTY
9781529148923	GOOD DAYS	1
9781035429042	HOW TO BE AN ADULT	1

Order IOq3EpV2r9

If your problem isn't major enough for A&E, and happens at the evening or weekend, you can probably find a walk-in centre, but it may be some distance from you. For years our family did not drive, so accessing urgent care was almost impossible on a Sunday, as the lack of buses meant we simply couldn't get there.

The other service is 111 – either ring or go online. As mentioned elsewhere, they are notoriously risk-averse. They will take your details and your number, then, if required, they will arrange for a clinician to ring you back. The clinician can either summon a doctor or an ambulance, or offer another solution.

What happens if someone is taken into hospital?

You may need to inform their employers, and see about sick pay if they are entitled to this. If they are on benefits that require them to search actively for work, make sure you inform the Department of Work and Pensions (DWP), as sudden silence may lead to the patient being sanctioned. If they are not able to deal with this side of things themselves, then you will need their name, date of birth and their National Insurance number. In my experience, staff can be either incredibly helpful and sympathetic or downright obstructive. If they are obstructive, then rather than lose your temper, try another route – you could visit the local Jobcentre and see if they can help, or simply ring back at a different time. If all else fails, then email AND write a letter, make a copy and send it by registered post. Both provide evidence that the DWP were informed, so they cannot try to claim they didn't have the relevant information in time.

If the patient has pets, then someone needs to take care of those animals properly. It will depend on the animals, of course – some cats are perfectly okay if someone goes in twice a day to feed them and empty any litter trays, but dogs may need to stay elsewhere, and at the very least will need walking two or three times a day. Try to get access to the property to ensure the fridge isn't full of food which will go bad, and make sure the electricity supply won't be interrupted if the person is on a pay-as-you-go system. Empty the bins, turn the heating down (unless any pets need it) but not off, and make sure the place is secure. Check regularly for post – a build-up of letters and junk mail is a good indicator a property is unoccupied, and it may become a target for burglars. Make sure the place is secure, perhaps put an upstairs lamp on a timer, and go in a few times a week just to make sure everything is okay.

Depending on why they are in hospital and how ill they are, you may need to take a few things in to them. Hospitals can supply the basics – toothbrush, toothpaste, towels and soap. However, one's own toiletries are always nice to have, along with either pyjamas or a nightgown, plus slippers and a light dressing gown if they are ambulatory. Bedside lockers are small, and sadly theft happens, so do not take anything valuable or too large.

Flowers are a no-no – they are not permitted on wards – but some snacks and a few nice drinks often go down well. Hospital tea is normally drinkable, but the coffee is instant, so I take coffee bags with me so at least I can have a decent cup of coffee. Reading material or a tablet or laptop loaded up with films is a good call, too, as the hospital TV service is expensive. Please remember that, although there will be free WIFI, they do not allow streaming or downloading, so as to ensure the network functions despite the many users. Hospitals have convenience shops where you can buy drinks and magazines, but they can be expensive, so I buy elsewhere. Smokers may take this as an opportunity to give up, as smoking is not permitted on NHS property.

If someone lives alone and is discharged, they may need a care package set up to ensure they have the care they need, but, obviously, funds are limited, so this may be

fairly sparse. Any queries are best asked of the ward clerk – they are not involved in clinical processes, but are the administrative person, so can usually direct you correctly. If you have been looking after the house, you might want to check they have basic groceries when they get out, such as milk and bread.

What happens if I am ill or taken to hospital?

Inform people who need to know: your employer, your housemates, or a friend who can check on the house and empty the bins. Organise someone to look after your pets – if you live alone, have a note in your purse about any animals that will need urgent attention.

You will be entitled to benefits of some description. Hopefully your job will give you sick pay, but, if not, the government should give you a basic income. I'm not going into details here, as these benefits change with time, so (once again) check the GOV.UK website for details. What you get will depend on your National Insurance contributions and your savings. If you are unwell for a long time, you will have a different route towards benefits. If possible, see if you can work from home – this depends on your job, obviously – because if you have to rely on government help, this may not be very much at all, and if it looks like you may be ill for some considerable time, you may have to look at your lifestyle to see if you can cut expenses drastically. Serious illness and disability can completely change your life in an instant, and if you have a few preparations made just in case, they will act as a buffer. If you are in a risky occupation, for example, you may wish to get some type of insurance cover.

For some longer-term health conditions, you may be entitled to Personal Independence Payments. This is a government benefit which is not means-tested: it's a monthly payment designed to help cover some of the costs involved in long-term disability. Be warned, though: it takes a long time to be processed, and frequently people are refused. If that happens, ask for a mandatory recon-sideration at once, as very often I suspect they count on you being too exhausted to go through the whole proce-dure again, but, on reconsideration, they will sometimes award you the money.

The worst thing about long-term illness is the realisation that you may never be the same again. It's tough – it's really tough. It could happen to any one of us, so if you are tempted to moan about disability legislation and complain about the expense of putting in ramps and lifts, please remember it could very easily be you.

Other types of help

If you are being threatened by someone, and feel you are unsafe, then that is what the police are for. If the threat is immediate, then phone 999. You will be asked if you need the Fire, Police, or Ambulance – and hopefully help will be with you quickly!

If you are out walking or running and think you are being followed, then bring up 999 on your phone, so that if someone does grab you, you only have to press dial. Or go into a pub or shop, if there is one nearby. I have also found going up to a door and fumbling for keys helps – if they don't then leave you alone, ring the doorbell, and if the door is answered, explain the issue. I've only had to do it once, in the days before mobile phones existed, but the poor man whom I disturbed was magnificent. He loudly greeted me as a best friend, invited me in REALLY loudly, and peered around for the follower, then we waited five minutes before I felt brave enough to leave. We did ring the police, but as the street was clear, that was merely a precaution.

Most people are kind, decent and helpful. Obviously some aren't, and it's damn near impossible to tell who is who, so exercise a little caution and try not to make a bad situation worse. But faced with someone who was extremely likely to be following me with ill intent and a random householder, I was happier with the house-holder!

11

SAFETY ISSUES

General safety: a little foresight goes a long way

Accidents happen, but many could have been avoided with a little forethought.

If you have children or elderly relatives living with you, I'm sure you are aware of trip hazards, the risk of pan handles protruding from a cooker and similar accidents in waiting. Health and safety isn't a joke. It saves lives.

There is always a sneer when people talk of health and safety, but the implementation of health and safety guidelines has saved a lot of lives. The principles are simple: identify risks and hazards in advance and try to eliminate them. This is something you can and should do in your daily life: you wear a seatbelt; you'd not dream of getting on a motorbike without a helmet, so why leave a candle unattended? Just take a second to think about safety – you don't have to become the safety bore, just be mindful of what you are doing, and if something looks hazardous, it's best to deal with it immediately or you'll forget.

Have a few spare keys cut and give them to reliable friends nearby (that fake rock is known to every burglar on the planet), and try to make sure those friends are likely to be around when you need them. The lovely old lady in the house opposite is a perfect person to hold keys, but will be deeply unhappy if you wake her at 3am after a night clubbing, so leave another key with a night owl who won't be shocked by your kebab-smeared face.

One neighbour of mine was a frightful drunk, and also a massive pain in the arse, so after a while no one would keep a key for him. In the end, he put a pillow and a blanket in the shed so that, if he locked himself out, he could crash there – a locksmith in business hours costs around £70, but one at 2am will set you back several hundred, and that's IF you can find one. Once he had sobered up, he could usually either find his key or get inside without help.

Hypothermia kills, however, even when it's not freezing. In fact, most deaths from hypothermia do not necessarily happen in sub-zero temperatures. Going to sleep drunk and wet on a spring evening when the temperature drops overnight can do it.

I went to the summer solstice at Stonehenge one year. It gets cold up there at 3am, and the staff on duty were frantically handing out plastic bags to people to serve as some small protection, and going around waking sleeping people in little clothing in case they were hypothermic. So, long story short, always take a jacket. I have one I use for cycling – windproof, showerproof and highly reflective, so I won't get hit by a car. It's small enough it packs down into a small bag, so it's easy to take out with me. Many a time I have walked home in the early hours – I was always grateful for a jacket, and the walk sobered me up nicely, so by the time I got home I was ready for bed.

Domestic violence and abuse

Why it's so hard to leave

Having been a victim of domestic abuse, I know how hard it is to ask for help. By the time the first punch lands, your abuser has usually got you psychologically bound to them. It's important, therefore, to teach our children about this, so they recognise a potential partner may be dangerous before they become too deeply involved.

Clare's Law – use it

We now have something called Clare's Law – the domestic violence disclosure scheme. You can make an application to the police to find out if a current or ex-partner has a record of domestic violence. You can ask if you are concerned about a friend or a family member, but the police may decide to tell them directly rather than disclose to you. If the person has no record, or the police believe they are no threat, they will tell you.

Love-bombing isn't love

Knowing what to be aware of in advance is important – and this is something teenagers should know, too, as they are often at risk. Please, PLEASE be aware of how coercion works. When you are young, it's so easy to be caught up by protestations of love and adoration, as it's flattering and makes you feel so treasured and warm. This can be something called love-bombing – and while it seems innocent and delightful, it may very well be a sign of something dangerous. Always talk to people – your friends, your parents, even safeguarding staff. It is incredibly easy to get caught up in strong emotions, to feel so desperately in love you cast off friends and family, especially if they express a concern about or dislike for your lover. You dismiss them as jealous and can be blinded by adoration. All this can be a sign that you are in an abusive relationship, not always, of course, but please be aware and keep communications going with others.

It often starts with meeting someone who very quickly declares you are their soulmate, and that they adore you. They shower you with love and affection; they appear to be the perfect partner. For a while, it is the perfect relationship. Over time, they start to get a little possessive, clingy; maybe they get upset if you choose friends or family over them, even for an evening. They point out how your friends are toxic, your family is difficult, but insist that they love you, and they will look after you.

Before you realise it, you don't have many friends and rarely see your family, but when you do, your abuser is charming to them – your parents think they are wonderful. You feel lucky having a partner so kind, so loving – it's just a shame you are both so busy and can't see your family more often.

If you do something they dislike, they become cold, they sulk. If you suggest you take a break, they threaten or attempt suicide.

You love them, so you stay.

Then they start breaking things when you argue, but they are sorry – you made them do it, they love you so much, you are their world.

Then they hit you. You try to leave, but they threaten suicide again. They threaten to hurt your cat – they even threaten you. People often look surprised if you tell them – but they're so charming, they say, so loving. The abuser tells people you are neurotic, slightly mad, but they love you and they put up with your terrible behaviour.

You stay – perhaps it was your fault, after all. Perhaps you don't love them hard enough, or perhaps you should be nicer? Perhaps you are slightly mad?

Then they try to kill you – but you can't leave, as they have control of your money, they can track your phone, and they've told you they will find you if you leave. They tell you they will kill you.

You stay.

You find yourself thinking: 'They didn't mean it.' 'They'll never do it again,' and 'It's only because they love me.'

But they do mean it, they WILL do it again – and, most importantly, that is not love.

There is help available – but you have to take the first step.

The police are great, and there are domestic violence helplines you can call – our local council even has numbers stuck in public lavatories. The National Domestic Violence Helpline number is 0808 2000 247, and they are available twenty-four hours a day. Ring them, talk to them. No one will think you are mad, and they will not take your children away. They will not lock you up. Tell your doctor, your child's school – take that first step, and you can be free of fear and thrive.

If you suspect abuse, speak up

If you believe a friend, your family member or neighbours are at risk of domestic abuse, then report it – don't turn a blind eye. It's better to report a potential problem than blame yourself for the rest of your life. People have died at the hands of an abuser. However, you cannot make a person leave their partner; they have been almost hypnotised into this position. All you can do is listen, offer support and be there if and when you are needed. On average, it takes seven attempts before someone successfully leaves an abusive relationship – it's not easy.

As a society, we need to stop allowing violence to go unchallenged. It is avoidable, and we can stop it.

Sounds of abuse can often be heard through walls, and even if you're not sure if it's abuse, it's better to report for safeguarding reasons. If there is a situation happening right now, dial 999 and tell the police. If it's not an immediate emergency, contact 101 – this is useful, as it begins a record. Police may not attend, but it may mean they have a note on the system, so if a 999 call comes in, they understand it to be part of an ongoing problem. If you are concerned about children or the elderly, you can contact social services for advice. It's important to remember that social services do not remove children from homes except as a last resort to ensure their safety – they aim to work with parents to provide a safe environment.

Addiction and debt: facing reality and finding help

I class these together, as very often spending is an addiction – just as gambling and cocaine are. There are plenty of organisations who can help, and if you are seeking help for a friend or family member, it's worth talking to them for advice and support – but the addict themselves is the one who must do the work.

StepChange, the debt charity, are the place to begin for debt – you'll find them online and they are brilliant at helping to find the best solution for you. Please deal with debt, as it makes your life so much easier if you do.

Dealing with the root cause of the addictive behaviour can be difficult, but it is achievable. There are lots of different organisations, with Alcoholics Anonymous probably being the best known. You may have to shop around a bit, as the AA model does not suit everyone. If you type 'rehab services near me' into a search engine, you'll get a mixed bag of results: lots of private clinics, some free council-run ones, plus a bunch of charities.

Private clinics are expensive, inpatient private clinics are extortionate, and to get long-term results, people need to stay for quite a while.

The charities are good. They are frequently staffed by people who are in recovery themselves, who understand the issues, and they can be brutal if needed. They are also very alert to the nonsense that people in active addiction come up with.

The local-authority-run clinics are variable – frequently the staff are completely overloaded and struggle to manage – but they can still be incredibly helpful when you engage and are honest. They will kick you off a programme if you don't abide by the rules, though, simply because it's a waste of time they could be spending helping someone else – so don't fanny around.

This is possibly the most important point to note – there is no magic fix for addiction. In order to treat it, you must engage fully – and getting to that point is challenging. Do not expect quick results. It requires a change of thinking and behaviour – you can dry someone out by force, but unless the underlying problem is addressed, the addiction is still there.

The takeaway from this is that recovery is possible, and there is life after addiction – it takes courage and determination, but you can have a good life if you are prepared to put in the work. Please don't give up – it's worth it.

Dangerous surroundings: what to do when your home or environment puts you at risk

Call Environmental Health

If you discover that your home is actively dangerous, that your neighbours are more than just irritating or that the local skate park is a death trap, you can feel trapped and worried.

The place to start is often the Environmental Health department of your local council. If you spy rats in your local takeaway, they are the people to ring – if it's not their area, they will usually be able to transfer you to the correct department. If you do deal with people on the phone, always get their email address and follow up with an email just outlining the call – it provides a paper trail to the correct department. This means that, if the person you spoke to leaves the agency, or forgets about it, you have got a record of what was said and when.

Dealing with anti-social neighbours

Antisocial behaviour is a matter for the police, so call 101 or report it online. You can do this anonymously if you prefer.

For ongoing problems, keep a written record – get a notebook and, every time the problem occurs, write it down. Include the date, the time and the issue. It might look like this:

Tues, 20th January, Mr X of no. 41 followed me for 30 foot calling me 'C8*t'.

Sunday, 25th, Mr X was playing loud music from 10.30pm until 3am, and when I asked him to turn it down, he threw a beer at me and called me 'C8*t'. Police were called but did not attend.

Tuesday, 27th, Mr X set light to his curtain. Fire service called.

This is evidence that shows the extent of a problem, and is accepted in court should that be required. It also makes it very difficult for any authority to dismiss you. Fill in interactions with authority as well, so that not only is a pattern of behaviour made clear, but your attempts to get help are also laid out.

Blackmail is a criminal offence – report it

If, for example, someone has a picture of you stark naked or doing something illegal and they try to extort anything from you, go to the police at once. Trust me here – you may feel like an idiot, but the blackmailer is the one in trouble.

Know your rights as a tenant

If your home is dangerous but you are scared of complaining in case you are evicted, then it is difficult. At present this does happen, but the best protection against exploitation from anyone is knowing your rights. As the law stands at the moment, you cannot be served a Section 21 ('no fault' eviction notice) within six months of making a written complaint about a genuine issue, such as a serious leak or non-functioning heating. So, firstly, write to your landlord. They then have fourteen days to either fix the problem or lay out plans to remedy the problem in good time. If that doesn't happen, report it to the Environmental Health department of your local council, who will then inspect the property and issue an improvement notice. If the landlord does do the repairs, they can then give you notice and evict you under Section 21 after six months have passed from the date of the improvement notice being issued, but if they try to issue a Section 21 earlier, the courts will not allow them to evict you.

For housing problems, Shelter are a charity with good resources and relevant knowledge, and Citizens Advice are also very good.

12

EDUCATION AND
EMPLOYMENT

The changing landscape of searching for a job

Finding a job has changed beyond belief since I last tried, and most jobs are now searched for online. You upload a CV and go through various screening processes. I'd be lying if I said I had any experience of this whatsoever, but I do know a few tips which can help.

Before you begin, think about what you'd like to do, and what you are able to do. If there is a job you'd like to do, but you don't have the necessary experience, there are often workplace training schemes where you spend some time learning on the job, and some time studying. The only problem with these is that they often don't pay much (as you are training), so look carefully at the wages and think about how you can manage it. But if you are keen, they can be a great way to get work in your chosen field. These schemes do change over time, so (once again) look on GOV.UK for the latest offerings.

Remember your transferable skills

You need to look at transferable skills – for example, if you've worked serving food at the local pub, you have good forward-facing customer-service skills. If you used the computer system to book tables and to revise orders, you are computer literate and those skills might easily take you into working in a reception role.

Tailor your CV to each job. Look at the role and the skills they are looking for and make sure these are clearly set out early on in your application. Keep things concise, as very often applications are automatically screened, and a fifteen-page essay on your scouting badges simply won't be read.

For less formal jobs – hospitality in a small town, say, or shop work for an independent retailer – you can still get results by walking in and asking. Pubs, for example, often put a note in the window when they have work available. This can be a great idea for a first job, or a term-time position while you are at uni. You will not find a job with a large company this way, but quite a lot of people I know in hospitality have started out with an agency doing temporary cover work, and then been offered a more permanent position, and it may well work this way with other industries.

Finding the right fit, for them and for you

While it's difficult to be picky if you are desperate for work, it's more likely you will be able to stay employed if the job is tolerable, or even enjoyable. If you need unemployment benefits, don't forget you can be sanctioned if you leave a job without good reason, and if you dip in and out of employment, an employer may not be interested, as they need a degree of reliability. Don't fall for that nonsense about how if you love your job, you never have to work a day in your life, as very few people indeed are in that position. We all work for the money we need to live. If we are very lucky our job is pleasant and pays us enough to live nicely, but many people work a difficult, demanding and badly paid job because eating and having a roof over your head costs money, so don't sneer at people in what you may see as menial jobs.

Job interviews: be prepared

If you are lucky enough to get an interview, make sure you do your research – know in advance what they are looking for, what the company do, and a few basics. Make sure you know what you expect to be paid. If the salary is vague, ask them to clarify exactly what they are offering – and, if it is too little, politely say that it's below what you were expecting, thank them for their time, then up and leave. It is possible they will increase the pay for the right candidate, so be polite and don't burn your boats! I would suggest, though, that you find out in advance what is reasonable and expected in that job – a company may pay slightly above what is normal for the right candidate, but they will not pay too much. Equally, it's important you know your own worth, and ensure that the hours and the pay offered reflect the skill and experience that you are bringing to the role.

Dress smart, stay clean

Dress appropriately for your job interview. The most important thing is to be clean and neat. If you're interviewing for an office role, wear a pair of clean, plain, well-fitting trousers, a nicely ironed shirt with a jacket and polished shoes. If you wear make-up, keep it toned down, and do not wear skin-tight clothes. Do not chew gum, and ensure your nails are unobtrusive. If the role is in hospitality or a similar field, wear a polo shirt and sensible, clean work shoes. Again. be clean and neat, with tidy hair and visibly clean hands and nails – if you're applying for a position working with food, ensure you have natural nails that are short and clean.

Be ready with your qualifications

Have details of any qualifications you have that are relevant, such as up-to-date tickets for site work.

Ask the right questions

Think about what questions you may be asked in advance, and be alert and polite. Look interested and make eye contact. Think about the question for a second before you answer. A good tip is to repeat the question in your head to be sure you are answering what they ask, and not what you think they are asking – it also stops you gabbling from nerves. Use this opportunity to ask any questions you have – about their pension scheme perhaps, or benefits, or why your predecessor left. And look out for red flags – phrases such as 'My staff go above and beyond,' for example. Ask them to clarify exactly what they mean by that. It often means they will expect you to come in early and work late and not be paid for it. Likewise, check about availability – are they going to expect you to cut short a holiday, or cancel a day off without warning? Pay and hours can sometimes be unclear. Are there a set number of hours per week, or per month? Is overtime expected or optional? Are you paid for work-related travel? Is there a probation period and, if so, how long is it?

Know your rights

Minimum wage – by law, many jobs, including part-time, agency and temporary work, must pay you the minimum wage. There are jobs for which the minimum wage does not apply, however, so please check in advance. The minimum wage is the minimum amount per hour that an employer can pay you, and it is a criminal offence if they are not paying you at least that amount.

This applies whether you are paid at an hourly rate or are on a salary. You are not paid for rest breaks, or travel to and from work, but your wages must be paid when you are at work or on standby, i.e. kept at the workplace but not working, because, say, a machine has broken down. You must also be paid if you are training, or travelling from work to training.

Keep your payslips

If you want to check if you are being paid correctly, there is good information and help on either the GOV. UK site or on acas.org. These sites have links to help you work out if your pay is correct, and they will help you to report your employer if you think they are not paying you enough. Employers must keep records for six years to prove they are paying people correctly. I always advise people to print out payslips if they are provided online, and if you are given hard copies, keep them. They are extremely helpful if you have a pay dispute in the future – for example, if your employer claims they have paid you more than they have, or if HMRC query your tax contributions.

Adult education: it's never too late to learn

Overcoming literacy struggles

Lots of people leave school with very few qualifications, and literacy rates are poor – 16.4% of people struggle with reading and writing. While I'll assume you can read comfortably, this statistic means you probably know someone who struggles. That is a huge disadvantage, and many people affected are ashamed. No one should ever be ashamed of what they don't know, so if you know people who struggle, let them know they can get help. Most colleges will have courses, usually functional maths and English for either native speakers or those with English as a second language, and they are often free or available at a low cost. It's well worth finding a class – apart from the sheer joy involved in being able to read fluently (books can be lifesavers), it can really pay off when job-seeking.

Learning for fun

Learning something new is a gratifying way to spend time – and anything is okay (although I would be happier if everyone stuck to factually accurate things – tell me you are studying homeopathy and I'll struggle to be polite). There are lots of online courses, books galore and your local college will usually have a wide offering of classes. The leisure courses are more expensive, but lots of people take them for a hobby. I know several pensioners with multiple Open University degrees – the cost has gone up considerably in the last fifteen years, but plenty of people study for the joy of it and would rather study art history than fly to Barbados.

When you study for fun, it doesn't matter what you study – but if you are trying to get usable qualifications, it's important they are valid and recognised, not just some random course on the internet.

Make sure your qualifications count

University degrees need to be accredited (officially recognised), and if you look at the university's prospectus, it should state whether or not they are. For UK universities, you can check on the Department of Innovation, Universities and Skills. Other countries also have accreditation bodies, but if you are studying in a different country to that in which you plan to work, it's wise to ensure your accreditation is recognised there. Please beware of internet universities that offer easy degrees and certificates for a fee; they are known as degree mills, and the certificates are worthless. Avoid private or for-profit universities, too – Wikipedia is worth checking if you're not sure!

If you're looking to get a professional qualification, you must check if the professional body for your chosen profession recognises the institution offering it, as there are far too many adverts for worthless qualifications from made-up organisations, often offering what seems like a bargain but absolutely isn't.

Consider alternative paths

You can get recognised and solid qualifications online – the Open University is a well-regarded university, and they offer everything from undergrad degrees to PhDs. They also offer technical qualifications, and what they refer to as micro credentials – short, industry-recognised courses around three months long.

Your local college will have courses, too, although the offerings can be a little limited if you are what is known as a mature student. They all put their prospectuses online, and some also offer online study, but mostly they require you to turn up in person, which means a lot of courses are in the evening to accommodate people who work.

If you are on a low income, you can potentially get help with the costs – just remember that many courses start in either March or October, so start applying early, especially if you are hoping for help with funding.

Think ahead before taking out a student loan

Student loans are available for quite a lot of this, but please be aware it IS a loan, and has to be paid back once you start earning over a certain amount a year, so try to be realistic about what you can expect to earn. When I left school, a degree was considered to be a way to ensure a good and well-paid job, but over time they have become less useful, and for many people a good trade qualification will be a better alternative.

Choosing the right degree for your career path

Some professions require a specific degree – law, medicine and nursing, for example. But do check if you are likely to be able to get a job in the field – a friend took a very expensive degree in criminal law and has been doing conveyancing work ever since, as she could not get the necessary pupillage to progress.

Other jobs are less exacting. They simply require you to have achieved a particular level of study, often referred to as a non-specific degree, which means it's irrelevant whether you have a BA in geography or history. The point of a non-specific degree is to show you are capable of study to a certain level, as you usually need to demonstrate you can guide yourself, think critically and keep to the deadlines given. That last one is remarkably important.

13

CIVIL AND CRIMINAL LAW

Staying on the right side of the law

It's not terribly difficult to stay on the right side of the law, and most of us have a basic understanding of it. It's very codified, but mostly involves not causing harm to other people or their possessions, not taking things that don't belong to you, and basically being a decent person. Financial fraud can be slightly more confusing if you are in business, however, so always look things up and get advice.

What to do if you are evicted without warning

I mentioned earlier that if your landlord throws you out without warning, you need to go to the police, but that they may say it's a civil matter (see p. 5): so, I'll make a slight digression here to explain this!

There are, broadly speaking, two types of law in England (Scotland has a different legal system, with which I am not familiar) – one is criminal and the other civil. Essentially, criminal law is concerned with punishment – if you break a criminal law, you are punished with prison, community service or a fine. It's the state who bring prosecutions, and the bar for being found guilty its quite high. Civil law is about a remedy – perhaps you want compensation, or someone broke a legally binding agreement. You cannot send anyone to prison, but you can claim monetary compensation or make them pay money they owe. It seeks to rectify an injustice. This is the type of law involved in contracts – it's between people or companies, and the burden of proof is lower, relying upon the balance of probabilities.

So the contract you have with your landlord is a civil matter, but if he kicks you out without warning, it is not only a breach of contract but a criminal offence. The police deal only with criminal law, but are also involved with keeping the peace – in other words, they can attend civil disputes, but only where a criminal law is likely to be broken. Usually, it's violence they seek to prevent – so, for example, if a bailiff attends to evict you, he may ask the police to attend to ensure his own safety and to check that everything is lawfully executed. That option is also open to you – if someone turns up on your doorstep claiming a legal right to entry, you can phone the police to a) check it is in fact a lawful entry, and b) to ensure your safety. I have found that if you politely refuse entry until the police attend, anyone who doesn't have that legal right goes away and doesn't return.

The right to entry: who can come into your home?

Many years ago, a very unscrupulous firm won a contract to collect debts. I forget who they worked for, but they did not have a right of entry unless you invited them in, whereupon they would just remove all your possessions, or they would get in through an open door or window. They employed large men in big coats, who turned up on your doorstep and told you they absolutely did have a right to enter, and that you should immediately let them in (in which case, they would remove all your possessions) or pay a vastly inflated sum of money, including several hundred pounds for the 'cost of attendance'. They were very menacing indeed and bullied me badly – even though I told them I knew they could not come in, they tried to push past me and were really very scary. I shoved the door closed and shouted through it that I was going to ring the police and ask them to attend, as I was frightened, with small children in the house, and said they should come back later when the police were there. I never saw them again, but I did ring the police, who very kindly agreed that if the men did return, they would be there quickly. A few months later, the firm ceased operating; I think there had been so many complaints they lost the contract.

The one bailiff who DOES have a right to enter is one with a warrant from the High Court – so if you are in legal trouble, make sure you deal with it before it gets to the High Court stage, as they can force an entry and either remove goods, or, in the case of eviction, you. Court fines and non-payment of council tax fall into this category, so make sure you pay those. I have seen various people crop up on social media waffling about how you cannot be made to pay council tax – ignore them, or there is a very real risk of you coming home one day to find your door has been unlocked and your telly removed.

Generally speaking, people who have a right to entry have a warrant, and you should be shown a copy of this, but there are some exceptions – notably the police, once they have arrested you, or if they are in pursuit. If you open your front door and are promptly arrested, the police absolutely have a right to enter and search your home. But the search can only be for things within the scope of what they are searching for. An example here is that if they are searching for a missing bicycle, they cannot start looking in your bedside drawers, as a bicycle could not possibly fit in them.

The arrest process: what to expect and how to cope

Hopefully you will never get arrested, but just in case you do, it's less frightening if you know the procedure. It is usual for the police put you in handcuffs to ensure their safety, after which they will place you in a secure compartment in the police car or van. They will then drive you to the nearest police station, where you will be handed over to the custody sergeant. They will give him your details, and details of what they wish to question you about, and at that point you will have your fingerprints and DNA taken. There is no point being anything other

than polite and courteous, as you will not win by shouting. If you think you need medical attention, inform the
custody sergeant and he will get a doctor to attend. They
will remove any belts, shoelaces and anything else you
could use to harm yourself or others. If you are very nice,
and very lucky, they might let you have a book to read,
but don't expect it. Then you will be escorted to, and
locked inside your cell. Officers will then go and prepare
to interview you under caution. They may go off to secure
more evidence, or they may just need to sort out the
paperwork. After that, you will be taken to an interview
room and asked if you want a solicitor – if you do, you
can either ask for one you know (who may bill you) or
they will appoint one for you. If you do require a solicitor,
they will return you to your cell until your representation
arrives. Then you will be interviewed under caution – this
is a verbal statement which is recorded in triplicate, and it
is admissible in court. You can refuse to answer any questions, and hopefully your solicitor will guide you through
this. If you have done nothing wrong, this may be a fairly
straightforward process, and sometimes you can clear
yourself – for example, if you've been arrested for assault
and the person shown on CCTV looks very like you, but
you were at work with lots of other people at the time.
Once the police have checked this out, they will allow you
to go. If they are not happy with what you say, and still

believe you have committed an offence, they have a few options. First, they can bail you under your own recognisance, then let you go home. If this happens, they may arrest you again, or phone you up to attend another interview. Alternatively, they may charge you. If this happens, they may want to put you on remand in prison while you await trial. This means you have to appear in court, then the court sets out certain details, and then you are taken to prison. They can also charge you and order you to turn up at court under your own steam. If you don't attend, though, they will look for you and arrest you, and then you will be held in custody until the next court date. All the above situations are dependent on how much of a danger you are, how serious the crime was, and how likely you are to come to court when told to do so. If you are aggressive, uncooperative and violent when in custody, they are far less likely to let you out. Likewise, if a condition of your bail is that you stay away from a certain person or place, then do as you are told.

Civil disputes and the role of a solicitor

They do charge, but usually you can get a short appointment with a solicitor for free where they can give you brief advice, outline fees and explain whether they think you will win. If you do win the case, it is usual that your legal fees are paid by the other side, but if you lose, you do have to stump up, so solicitors often ask for money upfront – not necessarily all, but some. This is why it's important to be honest with your legal counsel, as if you give the impression your case is an open-and-shut win, but you have concealed things which would complicate the situation, you could end up paying a large fee.

Contracts

ALWAYS READ CONTRACTS. Companies are not allowed to hide nasty things in their terms and conditions, but it's far better to read carefully and avoid surprises. As always, it's easier to prevent than to cure, especially if you've suddenly had money taken from your account. Be careful what you agree to, especially when it comes to verbal agreements – if it's important, get it in writing. For example, ask people to email you a confirmation of what you've agreed. It's important to ensure that you've agreed on the same thing, and if you only have a verbal agreement, it's hard to argue later on that, for example, when you agreed Brian

could have your lawnmower for his lawn, you intended him to return it, despite Brian claiming that when you said he could have it, you intended him to keep it.

Incidentally, while Brian will think you weird if you make him sign a contract to borrow your mower, it is wise to make it clear when you want it back. Just explain you'll need it by Wednesday, as your lawn will need doing by then. As a rule, never leave things open-ended.

14

THE POLITICAL PROCESS

I'm including this chapter as I was surprised by how many people did not understand how the UK political process works.

Why your vote always matters

The first thing you need to grasp is that when people try to tell you that your vote doesn't matter, they are almost always worried that your vote WILL matter, that it will affect them, so they think if they can persuade you not to vote, they will have a much easier time of it. Because while one vote probably won't affect things, it only takes a few hundred votes to change the entire course of a nation, and potentially the world. Don't believe me? In November 2000, George W. Bush and Al Gore both stood for election as President of the United States of America. They were pretty much neck and neck, with only Florida to be counted. After the first count, Bush had the lead by 327 votes out of 6 million cast. There was a lot of legal wrangling thereafter, but the result was that Bush was voted in. There is a lot more involved and, to be fair, a lot more votes would have been needed, but in a state who cast just under 6 million votes, a few thousand more people could have changed the world for ever. If you are interested, I suggest you look it up – it also shows that wrangling about electoral results has a longer history than some would have you believe. Al Gore was very keen on climate action – and can you imagine what a different world it would be now, had Gore become president?

Just 327 votes. Always vote, because it always matters.

The myth that all parties are the same

This is a notion put forward by those who would prefer you didn't vote. No matter which party is elected, they still have to do the same job: they will have to raise money through taxation and decide how to spend that money, and quite a lot of those decisions are not open to huge changes (after all, can you imagine what would happen if a new government decided to get rid of all the armed forces?). This can make it easy to pretend all governments are the same. It's true that, over the last twenty or so years, political parties have changed, however, and very often you will have to do some real thinking about who you wish to support. While I am not keen on our current system, as it has led to what, in practice, is a two-party system, you can only work with what is available.

I have for many years been of the opinion that the Green Party aligns best with my personal feelings, but I also know that the chances of the Green Party getting into power in the UK as it stands now are close to zero. So I make compromises, and you may well need to compromise too to get a government that is perhaps not what you want, but still better than the alternatives. This is something that became very obvious in the last election – many people were furious that the Labour Party set forward things in their manifesto that they disagreed with, as they felt that it was inexcusable for the party to become more centrist. The problem here is that, to enact any kind of change at all, a political party must first be elected.

They govern on behalf of everyone, not just you, and that includes the people you disagree with. In practice, this means they need to have policies in place for everyone, and some of those policies will be ones that you hate, but the man down the road will love – so, hopefully, everyone will get some things they like. It sounds like a cop-out, but while an opposition party can argue, and highlight the things the party in power is doing wrong, there is very little they can do to change it.

How the first-past-the-post system works

For our general elections (these are the ones that elect the government and which happen every five years), we use a voting system called 'first past the post' (i.e. winner takes all!). Basically, the country is divided up into constituencies, and each constituency elects an MP (a Member of Parliament) to sit in the Houses of Parliament, which is why they are referred to as 'seats'. The party who wins more than 50% of the seat forms the government, which is fairly straightforward, as if every MP votes in line with his party, they will win all the votes. If no party wins 50% of the seats, we have what is known as a hung parliament, as no party can guarantee to win every vote. What then happens in this instance is there is lots of discussion and then two parties or more will agree to form what is known as a coalition government.

This first-past-the-post system has its problems. The most serious one is that the government in power is often not truly representative of how the votes were cast, and therefore doesn't reflect what people in the country think. It does, however, mean that the government can govern decisively. This is not always the case with coalition governments, which are notorious for not getting much done.

What does the government do?

The main job of a government is to control the money supply, in that they set taxes, borrow if needed, and then decide where and how that money is spent. Running the finances of a country is not the same as running your personal finances, since the government can raise money from growth (a measure of how much money we are worth) and from how much is circulating around. Obviously, it costs money to run a country – roads, the military, pensions, benefits, the NHS – and the government decides how best to distribute the money it has. Governments also pass laws (called legislation), and these can drastically alter how we live. Although most probably won't affect all of us, they hopefully reflect how we as a country want to live. For example, it was illegal to 'practise homosexual acts' until 1967 in the UK, when England and Wales decriminalised it, but it remained illegal in both Scotland and Northern Ireland until the 1980s, reflecting the more conservative values prevalent in those two countries at the time. And it took until 2014 for gay couples to be able to legally marry. This was due to changing social attitudes. Different parties will have different values, and different takes on how they think we should live our lives.

Compromising in politics and the need for balance

In the run-up to an election, every party publishes a manifesto, which is a statement of what they believe in, and how they want to spend money and run the country. These are not legally binding, just a statement of intent.

Please bear in mind that small political parties often make big promises, ones they know they will never be called upon to fulfil. Be aware of this and try not to be seduced. You'd never hire a builder if he promised he could build you an extension for £500 and have it done within a week, so why try to elect a government who make equally empty promises?

Read manifestos carefully, and if you find them confusing, there are online tools you can use to find out which party you most align with. If that party doesn't really stand a chance of electing an MP in your area, but you are desperate for a change, then look at the party who is next in line – you'll have to make compromises, but hopefully that's something you can manage. If you absolutely hate your MP or the government, you may need to do what is known as 'tactical voting'. This is when you look at the person most likely to beat your current MP and vote for them, even if you dislike them – it's a case of the lesser of two evils. Look at their track record, too. If we return to our builder analogy, if he claims he can build that extension in a week, but he's been on *Rogue Traders* twice, once for trying to build a conservatory out of cheese, are you SURE you can trust him?

How election systems work elsewhere

Around the world there are other voting systems, the most popular one being something called proportional representation. This is not a single system but several different systems, which aim to ensure all parties have the appropriate number of MPs in line with the number of votes they got nationally. Both the Welsh and the Scottish parliaments use one of these systems. If you are interested, go to the website electoral-reform.org, as they have lots of resources explaining different systems.

One disadvantage of proportional representation, however, is that it often leads to coalition governments, so it can be hard to get things done. Another disadvantage is that it means virtually everyone gets some kind of representation, and that can include people with some very extreme political stances. It's one reason why some European countries end up with extremists in charge. Obviously sometimes that's fair, as in a democracy everyone should have a voice (although there is a point at which I'm not sure that holds true), but sometimes they hold a disproportionate amount of influence.

Local elections and their impact on your community

Not all elections are for the central government. We also have local councils, which are the administrative bodies that run counties, towns and cities, and they are elected separately from the government but also along party lines. They do not control money in the same way a government does, but can raise a levy known as council tax to fund local services – this is a mandatory tax, and you MUST pay it. They also get given money by the government, and some of that money comes with instructions. Not all of it, though, so please pay attention to council elections, as they can affect your day-to-day life a lot.

Your council organises the rubbish collection, runs social services, deals with roads and policing, and so much more. County councils have huge budgets and a lot of responsibilities, while town and village councils have far smaller budgets and their responsibilities tend to be limited to maintaining the local area, making planning decisions and anything else that is best dealt with locally.

How to make sure you're eligible to vote

Now you have a simple grasp of how things work, you need to be sure you can vote. Firstly, you must be on a list known as the electoral register. This is a list of everyone of voting age in the UK – it's a legal requirement to be on this list, but you can opt to have your information kept private. Where you live determines where you can vote, and you can only be on the register in one place – students can vote where they are at uni or at home, but they can only vote once!!

A step-by-step guide to voting in the UK

You will need photo identification to vote – a passport or a driving licence will do, but if you have neither of these, you can apply online for something called a Voter Authority Certificate, which is free. Please check that you have got the correct ID well in advance!

When an election is being held, you will get a poll card through the post giving you details of the place you need to go to vote. It's known as a polling station, and they are usually in town halls, church halls, etc.

Polls open at 7am and stay open until 10pm to ensure that everyone can vote, but they can get busy at peak times, so allow plenty of time, just in case you have to queue. You don't need to take your poll card, but you must have your ID.

When you get in, you will see several stations, and you must go to the correct one for your address. There will be people there to guide you, so if you are confused, please ask! They are a friendly bunch and will be delighted to help.

You will be asked your name and address, and then they will find you on a list. They will ask to see your ID and, if satisfied, they will draw a line through your name to ensure you can't vote twice. Then they give you your voting slip. ALL the slip has is a list of candidates' names, along with the party they represent, and next to each name is a box. You go to a booth, and you make a CLEAR 'x' in one box. Occasionally there will be two different elections held, and you must select more than one candidate – if this is the case, it will tell you on the slip. If you are confused, ASK. Look at the slip to be sure you understand, and don't rush.

Do not scribble out names or write rude comments, as slips that are not filled in properly are discarded, so you're not making a protest, you're wasting a vote. I've heard a lot about people taking their own pens, as usually the voting booths have pencils in them. You can take your own pen if you wish, but no one is going to rub out your cross. It's merely that pencils are reliable and low tech, and they are far less likely to spoil a vote than ink, which can smudge or smear.

You then fold your slip and put it into the ballot box.

YOUR VOTE IS PRIVATE. There is nothing on the slip to identify you, and you do not have to tell anyone who you voted for if they ask. There are often people doing exit polls outside, and they may ask who you voted for, but it's up to you if you tell them – and if you have reason to, you can lie, as no one will know.

Being an informed voter: what to watch out for

I hear often about people disliking how the country is run, and there are lots of inflammatory posts on social media, some that have even led to rioting. Firstly, we know many social media accounts are run by foreign interests who want to destabilise our government, and every government. Remember that not everything you read online is true – in fact, an awful lot is outright lies. And print media is no better, as most of it is owned by very rich men who want their media outlets to reflect their personal wants and desires. If you believe a billionaire has the same priorities as you, then you are mistaken. At present, Reuters and the Associated Press are probably the most accurate and least biased sources of news (if you're interested, there are charts online you can use to see how accurate and biased an outlet is).

However you vote, please be sure your decision is based on solid facts, not wishful thinking or fantasy. There are various news outlets spreading woeful and dangerous lies, and many more who are misleading. They publish big, splashy headlines knowing people rarely read further, and if they are called upon to correct something, you can be sure the correction will be in tiny print, buried deep inside the paper. Be aware of this, and don't let yourself be manipulated. Try to vote not just for yourself but for other people – your children, or the homeless chap on the bench, for example. Think about what kind of society you want to live in and vote in line with that.

Getting involved in politics: from voting to representation

If you are unhappy about the way things are run, either at a local level or just in general, think about becoming involved. To start with, you could join a political party – there's a monthly subscription involved, and that's used to help fund running the party. Or maybe you could start turning up to council meetings to see how things are done? You can even stand for election. If there is a vacancy on your parish council, then ask about filling it. It does take time, but you do get paid, even if it isn't a lot, and you must take it seriously. Standing as an MP is a more difficult process, and involves you first being very involved with your party. Then, if you indicate you may be willing, and they agree you are a suitable candidate, they can put you forward. Politics is for everyone, as it affects everyone, so if you are interested, please get involved.

15

EMERGENCIES

What to do when things go wrong

Hopefully you will never encounter a true emergency. If you ever do, it is easy to feel paralysed and scared. But most such scenarios are vanishingly rare. I've never come across a serious traffic accident before the emergency services are present, for example, but I have a rough idea of the steps involved, so hopefully, if I'm ever in that situation, I'll remember the key points. It's awful when people desperately need help and you don't know what to do . . .

Very often people have the necessary skills, but they are so shocked they freeze and fail to act. You can prevent this by knowing in advance the very basic first steps. You will also notice that quite a bit of the advice here focuses on NOT getting into trouble in the first place, as so much can be prevented by a little forethought – it costs thousands every year to bring out the coast guard or mountain rescue to people who honestly thought walking off path on a mountain in trainers and a T-shirt was a good idea. Be aware of potential hazards and avoid them, as it's not just your own life you are putting at risk

Please remember that untrained well-meaning bystand-ers can cause real problems for the trained responders, so PHONE EMERGENCY SERVICES FIRST. Very often they will guide you through what needs to be done, but occasionally immediate action needs to be taken.

So, take a deep breath and work out what MUST be done immediately, and what is best left to trained pro-fessionals. For the vast majority of the time, all you need to do is stop people dying before help arrives, but if you cannot get help at once, you may need to do just a bit more. So, if you aren't being advised by emergency services, take things one step at a time.

Delegate if you can, as very often other people are perfectly able to be of assistance, but you just need to jolt them in to action. Bark orders to people, i.e. 'You! Man in red, phone the ambulance! Woman in green, put that person in the recovery position! I am doing CPR here.' Most of the time, people will either oblige or look scared, in which case someone else may step into the breach. Bystander effect is a real thing, so break the spell!

Is everyone breathing? Are they in imminent danger of death? That won't wait. Do you know first aid? Does anyone else? Who is in the most danger?

This is called triage, and it's what happens every time you have a medical emergency and either phone 999 or turn up at A&E. Basically, people who are at risk of imminent death are dealt with first. It's why the wait times at A&E can be so long, as even if you are in significant pain, as long as you are not on the verge of death, you can wait. But once you stop breathing, say, you can be dead in moments.

It's always handy to have done a first-aid course to learn the basics, but if you haven't, and no one else is there, then you still have to do something! If someone has stopped breathing, they will die unless you intervene, so you cannot make things worse.

What are the five steps of first aid?

DANGER. Before approaching the casualty, always make sure the area is safe.

RESPONSE. Check if the casualty is responsive or unresponsive.

AIRWAY. Next, you need to check that the airway is open and clear.

BREATHING. You now need to check if the casualty is breathing normally.

CIRCULATION. Check their pulse.

Remember that your job isn't to fix someone; you are merely keeping them safe and alive until trained people arrive, so, as I've said, phone the emergency services first. The people on the end of the phone ARE trained, and they will tell you what to do, so listen to them!! I am listing some things below, however, in case emergency services are not available for some reason.

If the person is not breathing, then it's time for CPR! Start this even if someone has run off for the defibrilla- tor. Firstly, roll the person onto their back, pull their chin up and sweep your finger around their mouth to clear any obstruction. Check if they are breathing; if NOT, perform thirty chest compressions, followed by two rescue breaths. This is brutal but saves lives, so learn what to do today.

If someone is breathing and in no further danger lying where they are, put them in the recovery position. Cover them with a coat or blanket if you think they need it.

If someone is bleeding and there is nothing sticking out of the wound, make a pad with something (your shirt, perhaps) and apply firm pressure to slow the blood. If there is anything sticking out, DO NOT REMOVE IT, but apply pressure around it – you're aiming to slow blood loss.

If someone is crushed under a weight, don't lift it off them – try to support the weight so it does no further damage, but lifting the weight clear can cause their blood pressure to drop dangerously fast, so it's better to wait for the emergency services.

Choking

Choking is often SILENT. It happens when someone's airway is blocked, and they cannot breathe. It's an emergency and won't wait.

Firstly, check the person's mouth. Run a finger around to check for food or a foreign body you can pull free – if so, be careful not to push it further down

For a child or baby, lay them face down over your lap with their head lower than their hips, and hit them firmly and sharply between the shoulder blades – you're aiming to force air from the lungs, to push the obstruction free.

In adults, try the Heimlich manoeuvre: stand behind the patient, put your arms around them, clasp your hands together, then place on the solar plexus, which is at the top of the inverted V shape formed by the ribs. Pull hard and sharply in and up – it's the same objective as before, as you're trying to pop the blockage out.

If you are a tiny person with short arms, you might not manage this on a massive person, so instruct a larger, beefier person to try!

Keep going until the ambulance arrives – this is another situation where, if you do nothing, they will die, so you cannot make things worse.

Electrocution

Electrocution is far less common today, due to good breaker circuits, but the most important thing to remember is that, if someone is still connected to the electric current and you touch them, you too will be electrocuted. Use a non-conductive object to push them free – a wooden broom handle or a plastic bin, say, but obviously nothing made from metal. Then check they are breathing, etc.

If the person is close to a high-voltage source, such as an electricity substation, keep well clear and DO NOT APPROACH. They are probably dead, and you will quickly join them if you get too close. It goes without saying (I hope) that 'High Voltage: Keep Out' signs should always be obeyed. Some of us remember the terrifying public information films from the 1970s, which explained that electricity can jump quite a distance.

Fire

Fire is noisy, terrifying and moves fast. Domestic fire equipment is designed to stop a small fire growing. If a fire starts and cannot immediately be extinguished, then CLOSE THE DOOR on it and get everyone outside quickly while you summon the fire service.

Once you are out of the house, and if you can do it SAFELY, turning off the gas supply can be a good idea.

Do not try to save your possessions. If you are trapped and cannot get out, then get low, close as many doors as you can between you and the fire, and stuff things under the door to try to block smoke. You can also put a cloth over your mouth.

Before disaster strikes, it pays to walk around your house and flat and think about how you could escape a fire, as when you are scared, your brain doesn't function very well, so having a pre-thought-out plan in place could save your life. Double-glazed window panels, for example, are unlikely to break if you hit the middle with a chair, but smack a corner sharply with a metal stiletto heel and they may shatter. Perhaps a fire-escape ladder could/should be stored under a bed just in case? Don't make yourself paranoid, but a few minutes spent working these things out in advance can be invaluable when you are under pressure.

Most vitally, make sure you have WORKING smoke alarms, test them regularly and NEVER take out the batteries for another appliance. The same goes for carbon monoxide monitors – test them regularly, as they save lives daily. I also keep a fire blanket and a small powder fire extinguisher in my kitchen, so if needed I can put out a small fire before it grows.

Fights and riots

Don't try to break up a fight, as people have died trying. Just move others away, try to keep children out of sight, and stay calm. Half the energy in a brawl is fed by the excitement of onlookers. Fights can grow and turn into something far nastier, so keep well clear, and try to keep others clear – yelling and screaming does nothing at all. Phone the police if it looks serious. I've added riots to this, as, while I write this, there has been rioting up and down the country. If you hear chatter, online or in person, of people planning violent disorder, please report it using the online 101 tool, rather than the phone. It IS a crime to incite violence. If an actual riot breaks out nearby, STAY INSIDE. Do not go out to look. It's the same as with fights – you risk feeding the energy. There is a real risk of injury if a riot is underway, and the police will have to spend time trying to protect you when they could be containing the violence. Keep children and pets inside, and obviously consider giving shelter to anyone caught away from home or possibly injured. If there is a vulnerable person living alone nearby, and you can SAFELY do it, consider either going to them, or bringing them to yours. You can keep each other company and, hopefully, stop each other from being as scared as you might otherwise be. Other than that, stay inside, behind locked doors, and draw the curtains if there is a risk of your windows being smashed, as this will contain the glass. If you think it's wise, go upstairs. There's no need to phone emergency services, as it's better to keep the lines clear, or the operators will be overloaded.

If you wish to help with the clean-up next morning (something we as a society are good at doing), then please wear stout shoes and thick gloves – a mask, too, if there has been burning. Tea, coffee and good cheer always help! You'll be far more useful the next morning than you could possibly be as an audience. It also helps to remind everybody locally that the majority of people are decent and kind, and that you pull together as a community when needed. Children and the elderly especially need to be reassured that they are safe and that the bad people have gone away. Most people on the planet are decent and kind, so do not let yourself forget that fact!

Floods

If you are in your car, please be careful driving through flood water, as it is possible to wreck a car in fairly shallow water. If you are totally certain your car can manage it, then drive slowly and steadily through; keep your foot on the accelerator and keep going. As soon as you emerge fully, tap your brakes several times before picking up speed. If you do stall the car, be careful trying to get out, as even seemingly shallow fast-moving water can pull you off your feet. If you get swept away, you can easily end up drowning.

If your car starts to sink, then undo your seat belt and open the door or window as soon as it starts to go down. It seems counterintuitive, but the weight of water pressing onto a door can make it impossible to open, and obviously the circuitry in windows won't work when wet. Just kick yourself free of the car as fast as possible. People float – cars do not.

If you live somewhere where flooding is likely, and you suspect water might enter the house, act ahead of time and move things upstairs in an attempt to preserve them. Important paperwork can be sealed in plastic and kept on hand, so that if you must evacuate, it's ready and waiting.

If you live near a river that regularly breaks its banks, you may get a fair sense of when it will go and so have a few hours to prepare the house. We had severe flooding about twenty-five years ago, and one of our neighbours got a foot-high plate welded across his doorway. Although most of the time it's a nuisance having to step over it, in the last few years it's been invaluable. Be aware that with the onset of climate change, severe weather events are becoming more frequent.

The most important thing, though, is life. If you have been told to evacuate, grab your phone, charger, wallet, keys and the cat, and make tracks pretty damn quick. Remember to put the dog on a sturdy lead. I live in dread of having to evacuate into a hall with other pets, as my dog Hollie is a growly wreck with other animals. NEVER risk sacrificing your life or that of rescuers for material possessions.

If you live in an area at risk where no evacuation order has been given but you have reason to worry flooding might occur, grab your children and your animals, quickly put on suitable clothes and make for higher ground. And, as mentioned, do not try to cross flowing water unless it is extremely shallow, as water only a few inches deep can pull you off your feet.

Burglary

Make sure your doors and windows have robust locks that are engaged at night, as well as when you go out. I advise a thumb-turn release on the inside of a door, as, in an emergency you don't want to waste precious moments searching for your keys to get out.

If you do not have one of these, make sure the door keys are ready to hand and always in the same place, but not visible through a window or a letter box. I think the idea of burglars fishing for keys through the letterbox was overplayed, but it's best not to chance it.

Don't advertise your valuables. For example, remember that if you buy an expensive and portable item, the empty box put out for the rubbish is a fairly good indicator that the item lies within your home. Draw curtains when you put the lights on, and while everyone wants their home to look nice, it might be unwise to draw attention to the fact that you may own more than your neighbours. It's often considered rude or vulgar to flaunt things, but it's unwise too. Many years ago, I lived in a very smart part of London, and my house, while shabby and rundown-looking, had within a large amount of expensive electrical gadgetry. My two nearest neighbours, meanwhile, had beautifully decorated exteriors, and expensive curtains in the windows – one was burgled seven times in two years, the other five. We weren't touched, and I suspect it was simply because it wasn't apparent there was anything worth taking inside.

There are two schools of thought regarding what to do in the event of an active burglary – say, if you wake up and hear an intruder rifling through your drawers. One is to make noises to alert them to your presence, and, to be fair, most burglars will leave at that point; however, this strategy can be dangerous, as they may come upstairs to silence you. Generally, I prefer the second option, where you just quietly dive under the covers and dial 999 on your mobile. Don't use a landline, if you have one, as the downstairs extension might chirrup to alert them.

Death

I have covered a natural and expected death elsewhere (see p. 199), so this is just what to do if you come across an unexpected or possibly suspicious death.

If you come upon a sudden or violent death, it's a shock, so try to pause and take stock before you rush into action. If there is even the smallest chance of foul play, it is vital nothing is disturbed, so do not approach – just stay well back and phone the police. Equally, finding someone who has been dead for a while can be grizzly in the extreme, so, again, pause and call the police. This is a situation where you will need counselling, so seek it out quickly.

If you think there is a chance someone may be alive, then approach gently and check, but touch them as little as possible, and then phone for an ambulance, and the police too.

Trouble in the great outdoors

Every year, people get into trouble while enjoying the great outdoors, and very often it's because they were completely unprepared and ill-equipped. Avoid this by being sensible.

If you are out walking, wear suitable footwear (trainers are NOT suitable for hill-walking, for example) and make sure your phone is charged. Wear a light backpack and bring with you a snack and enough to drink, along with anything else you might need. I like to carry a wind-up torch and a rape alarm, not because I expect to be attacked, but because it's louder than I am, so is a good way to attract attention. A whistle works just as well, as it should attract every dog for miles . . . That said, if you want to attract a Labrador, hide behind a bush to pee – one will arrive in moments, I often find.

I'd also advise having a coat. The latter is ultra-important if you are walking in hills or mountains, as weather systems move in quickly. It's common to go out in a light T-shirt and shorts because it is hot and sunny, and an hour later find yourself caught up in thick cold fog. I always carry a lightweight disposable poncho when out in the summer. It only cost £1, but even a bin liner with slits for your arms and head can be a lifesaver. It prevents the wind wicking away heat, and obviously helps keep you dry.

I suggest installing the What3words app, if you haven't already. It works globally and gives rescuers a very precise location, which is essential, especially if you are off-road. And if you use SMS to alert someone as to your whereabouts, then stay put!

Wear bright clothing so you can be spotted from the air, and always, always make sure people know where you are going. Give them a rough ETA and, if things change, just let them know – a text message will often get through even if the signal is poor.

If you are in a hot country, you will need plenty of liquid, sunscreen and a hat – and don't just decide to hike a small, unknown path. If you feel unwell, seek shade and RING FOR HELP. Don't risk heat exhaustion by straying further; just keep hydrated and wait it out in shade, even if that shade is your T-shirt pulled over your head as you curl up on the path.

While our phones are great for navigation, they can run out of battery or lose signal – so take a paper map and a compass, or just print one out if you are reluctant to buy a full map. Or, if you really can't bear even that, at least either download or screenshot the directions.

If you slip and hurt yourself, or become lost, DO NOT WANDER OFF. Stay put and phone for help. Give the operator your What3words location and STAY WHERE YOU ARE. If you cannot get a signal, try to backtrack a bit until you can, but do not leave the path.

At sea or on water in general, please always wear a life jacket. Make sure your children wear them, too, and put one on the dog – I don't care if you aren't planning on going far out, just wear one. Check to see if it has a whistle attached – the sound from a whistle carries further than you shouting, and you're far less likely to take in a lungful of water too. Put your phone in a waterproof pouch – and, as before, install What3words before setting out. If you find yourself in trouble, ring the emergency services and ask for the coast guard. Stay with your boat or float, as they are far easier to see from a distance. Once again, wear bright colours – pinks, bright yellow or scarlet – as you need to be visible, especially when underwater, so blue is a no-no. NEVER let children muck around with swim rings or lilos unless you are right there, preferably hanging on to a tether, as they can be swept off quickly.

Learning to swim is an essential skill, but now public baths have mostly closed it can be difficult to find a pool. If you have access to one, please consider getting swimming lessons for yourself and any children you might have. Being able to swim does not mean you can ignore the previous safety recommendations, though – it just adds a layer of extra safety.

Traffic accidents

First things first: ensure that everybody is in a place of safety. Get them off the road, if appropriate, and if people can safely be moved. Stop traffic if people cannot be moved. If there is a biker on the ground, leave them exactly as you find them, please, as a broken neck is a real possibility. Phone the police and mention an ambulance is also needed.

Never remove a bike helmet, as you can paralyse the rider if you do. Unless people are at risk, then leave them in situ – just reassure them help is coming. Obviously, as before, your aim is to stop people dying, and as you will have phoned emergency services, you'll have expert advice on the line to help you judge whether someone needs immediate help.

Do not offer them anything to eat or drink until the ambulance service has cleared it, as people might need to be anaesthetised, so just leave them.

CONCLUSION

Hopefully this book helps a little. I've tried to fill it with everything I want my own children to know, things I think are either essential or simply useful. Adult life is a minefield, so please remember that most people you think of as responsible and together are just winging it. You will make mistakes, and you'll make them a lot – we all do. Do not trust people who claim to have all the answers, as they really don't – sure, most people have a limited area of expertise and also experience, but ask them anything outside of that and they are lost. Be open to learning and give yourself some grace. Extend that grace to others too – not for them, but for you. Protecting your peace involves not allowing yourself to be upset by the actions of others. After all, the only person you can control is yourself.

My qualifications for this book are a lifetime of having little money, and having worked in all sorts of professions – hospitality, housekeeping, cooking, making and selling crafts and plants, and, last and very definitely least, selling shoes. I was truly terrible at selling shoes, but it did teach me a bit about leather goods. What I have learned overall is that you learn a lot by asking – and that there are organisations that have been set up to help. All mistakes within these pages are my own (and possibly my grandmother's, but she died in 1987, so is past blame).

Acknowledgements

This book is dedicated to the oncology team at Salisbury, Southampton and Poole without whom I would not have been able to write.

Your cheerful and unfussy kindness makes a real difference to the lives of so many people, from endless cups of tea, to gently holding hands. From cleaners to consultants you do an amazing job, giving people hope and dignity until the very end.

I would also like to thank my editor Anna Steadman and the staff at Headline for putting up with my scattiness, and friends and family who astound me daily by not giving in to the desire to murder me.

Useful links/resources

For almost everything, start with any Google hit with a .gov.uk suffix, as that will tell you it is a site run by the UK government, meaning it will be up to date and lawful. Then read on.

For housing-related problems – Shelter.org

For help with general legal issues and wise, far-ranging advice – Citizensadvice.org.uk

For help with employment law and workplace relations – ACAS.org.uk

For help with local issues, including noise complaints and housing, and the social services for your area, phone your local council. Ask which department you need or look online.

For help with VAT or tax issues, phone HMRC, as I've found they're easier to phone and will bend over backwards to help.

For help with consumer issues – Tradingstandards.uk

For help if you are a child, or are concerned about a child's welfare – Childline.org

For help regarding the general welfare of both adults and children, contact your council's social services department – they may not be the people you need, but they will signpost you to the right place.

The NHS website (nhs.uk) has good, clear and up-to-date information about health-related matters.

Index

RAISING READERS
Books Build Bright Futures

Dear Reader,

We'd love your attention for one more page to tell you about the crisis in children's reading, and what we can all do.

Studies have shown that reading for fun is the **single biggest predictor of a child's future success** – more than family circumstance, parents' educational background or income. It improves academic results, mental health, wealth, communication skills and ambition.

The number of children reading for fun is in rapid decline. Young people have a lot of competition for their time, and a worryingly high number do not have a single book at home.

Our business works extensively with schools, libraries and literacy charities, but here are some ways we can all raise more readers:

- Reading to children for just 10 minutes a day makes a difference
- Don't give up if your children aren't regular readers – there will be books for them!
- Visit bookshops and libraries to get recommendations
- Encourage them to listen to audiobooks
- Support school libraries
- Give books as gifts

Thank you for reading.
www.JoinRaisingReaders.com

Ann Russell – a self-described 'middle-class English old bag' – is a self-employed cleaner who recently found fame (and 2.8 million followers) on TikTok, where she regularly shares cleaning and general life advice. Affectionately named 'The TikTok Auntie' by commenters, Ann films hundreds of video clips every month, answering questions on everything from tackling laundry stains to dealing with grief.

By Ann Russell and available from Headline

How to Save Money

How to Clean Everything

Ann Russell

HOW TO BE AN ADULT

Everything you need to know
about being a grown-up,
from bills to break-ups

This book reflects the opinions and advice of the author.
It is not intended as a substitute for professional advice.
Readers are strongly encouraged to consult qualified professionals
regarding their mental and physical health. The author and publisher
are not liable for any losses, damages, or consequences
resulting from the contents of this book.

The right of Ann Russell to be identified as the Author of
the Work has been asserted by her in accordance with the
Copyright, Designs and Patents Act 1988.

First published in 2025 by Headline Home
An imprint of Headline Publishing Group Limited

1

Cataloguing in Publication Data is available from the British Library.

Hardback ISBN 978 1 0354 2904 2
ebook ISBN 978 1 0354 2905 9

Illustrations © Ruth Craddock

Designed and typeset by EM&EN
Printed and bound in Great Britain by Clays Ltd, Elcograf S.p.A.

Headline's policy is to use papers that are natural, renewable and recyclable products
and made from wood grown in well-managed forests and other controlled sources.
The logging and manufacturing processes are expected to conform to
the environmental regulations of the country of origin.

Headline Publishing Group Limited
An Hachette UK Company
Carmelite House
50 Victoria Embankment
London EC4Y 0DZ

The authorised representative in the EEA is Hachette Ireland,
8 Castlecourt Centre, Dublin 15, D15 XTP3, Ireland (email: info@hbgi.ie)

www.headline.co.uk
www.hachette.co.uk